Runaway Mind
My Race with Bipolar

by

Maggie Reese

I wrote this book for everyone who suffers from Bipolar Disorder.

I dedicate this book to my sweet and lovely daughter, Allison,

and the love of my life, Matt, my bodyguard.

3

CONTENTS

Chapter 1

HOME

I will never forget the fall of 1995. Everything I knew to be normal was changing and changing drastically. I was packing my life in three boxes and moving one thousand miles away from home. Although I was nineteen years old, and more than ready to go away and start a new life, something deep inside me was not quite right. I was scared. Though I knew that many kids my age were going off to college like me, I did not want to go.

I grew up on a beautiful ranch in Jamestown, California. I had just finished my senior year at Sonora High School. I had done well with my academics and had done especially well with my athletics. In fact, I had set every Sonora High School record for cross-country and track in middle distance running, including the section title for both cross-country and track. I came in ninth statewide, which was a major feat in California, the most populous state in the nation.

Even at that, I had a feeling I was just getting started. I knew I had a lot more to give in my college career. I had not even scratched the surface yet.

I dreamed big. I dreamed of the Olympics. I had something special in me in my life, and I knew I had to show everyone who I was. I dreamed of being a running model for Nike clothing, doing commercials, getting into the movies; I knew nobody could stop me. I was not only a star athlete, but was also a beautiful 5'9" blonde whose athletically tuned physique was in itself a work of art. I was Maggie Hurst—watch out! My triumphs just seemed to keep coming. I got offers for scholarships across the country for running. UCLA, Berkeley, Baylor University, Texas, Arizona, San Diego State, Oregon, Washington State, just to name a few. I chose the University of Idaho. I liked it because it had a good running program at the time, it was not a huge school, it looked like a fascinating place and was just enough out of the way; and Dad had gone there and loved it, so I thought, why not? It was such a beautiful school with huge brick buildings covered in ivy, and the sky was so big—there was so much space! I liked that a lot since I was from such a small town. I felt I was not ready for the big cities yet. I knew that would come later. I had to prove myself in a small college first and then ease into the big time. My self-confidence seemed to be at an all-time high; I knew I would wipe out the big schools with my running. I would be the beautiful tall blonde from Idaho that would crush the world.

Even so, I could never forget my wonderful girlhood on the Hurst ranch. My brother, Tom; sister, Amy; and I were so lucky to grow up on sixty acres where we could run and play. I remember venturing off in the morning and not coming home until it began to get dark. At night, we would lie under the stars on the deck while Mom would tell us stories and locate constellations. During the day, I would play with my best friend, Carrie. We would build forts and pretend to be under attack. Then we would saddle up the ponies and go for adventures on what we called the Big Mountain. Jamestown would get hot during the summer, so one of our favorite things would be jumping off the rocks into the pond at the creek. We were never bored. We would put pennies on the railroad track for the antique steam locomotive to flatten when it came bustling through from the Rail town historic park. Sometimes, just chasing cows or herding sheep was enough to entertain us. We used to float on handmade rafts and pick blackberries until our hands were stained a reddish purple. Then we would take our buckets to Mom, and she would make the best blackberry pies.

I had so many wonderful memories of growing up in the country, that it was hard to leave despite my big plans for the future. The fun I had growing up on the ranch was endless, and now I would be leaving that special place. I would be leaving Mom's delicious ranch meals, Dad making funny conversations at the dinner table, and Thomas—whom I had sibling battles with, played with, and became great friends with all through high school. Amy was five-and-a half years older than I was, so I did not see her that often at this time in my life.

But I still felt I was leaving her behind too. She had come to many of my races.

I especially remember her at my section title race in Sacramento in my junior year. She gave me flowers and a big hug I will never forget.

I could not help but think of my childhood as Mom and I left for Idaho on a beautiful September day. As I gave my best friend, Carrie, a hug, I felt a tug at my heart. My life was really going to change. Carrie and I had been "tied at the hip" since second grade. How was I going to live somewhere without her? She was going to Chico State in our home state California. I was moving two states away. I felt like crying right there, but I kept up a brave face and gave hugs and kisses to my dad, my brother, and my sister. I knew I could make it through; my sister, Amy, went to college, and she did great. So off in the blue Blazer we went. It felt as though we were in slow motion going down the driveway.

Looking back at the ranch house, I realized things were never going to be the same. I was leaving such a wonderful childhood, and I was growing up. It never occurred to me how much I loved the ranch until I was leaving it for the first time. As soon as the Blazer turned out of the ranch gates, I felt a tear slide down my cheek. I quickly brushed it away so Mom could not see. I had to be brave and show her I was becoming an independent young adult. Let's face it, my childhood was fading away. Before we got to the University of Idaho, we went to go visit my grandma in Pasco, Washington. My Uncle Steve and Aunt Pat also lived close by in Mesa. We all met up at Uncle Steve's ranch. His ranch, the Hailey Ranch, was big and made the one I grew up on look like a speck. Mom had grown up here and had a terrific childhood. She went to Washington State and had met my father at a small bar in Moscow, Idaho, when he was attending the University of Idaho.

It was great to see my grandma, aunt, and uncle, but I did not feel like myself. For the last couple of weeks, there was a hot spot on my lower back that kept hurting. As we were all chatting about my plans at Idaho, the spot really started to burn. I excused myself to the bathroom to take a look at it. When I lifted my shirt, the spot looked like a massive cyst. I had to do something for relief, so I wrapped tissues around my fingers and squeezed the swollen lump.

The pain was excruciating, but the pressure was relieved, and large quantities of pus came out of it, followed by blood. When I finally came out of the bathroom, everybody asked me if I was all right because I looked pale. I didn't answer and sat down in a daze. I showed Mom later that night, and she said it was a boil and that you get them from stress.

NOTE: As we learned in the foreword, stress can be a major trigger for anxiety and depression. Physicians indicate that reactions to stress can manifest physically as well as psychologically, and both types of symptoms can occur at the same time. Maggie and her mom intuitively read the symptom correctly.

I felt that boil was a sign that something bad was going to happen. That evening, I dreamed strange dreams of faces that I didn't know in a cold, dreary place with snow whirling about, so I couldn't place anyone or anything. I woke up in a cold sweat and wiped my brow, telling myself I was okay. I stared into the darkness for what seemed liked an hour. I couldn't stop thinking about that boil in my back and my dreams. I didn't feel right, but did not know why. I couldn't shake the feeling that something very frightening was ahead of me, but I didn't know what that was. Finally, I drifted off to sleep.

NOTE: One difficulty with psychological illnesses is that they seldom manifest all at once. It is a process—and so, those who are slipping into bipolar behavior may simply feel that, in the early stages, they are suffering simple moodiness. Health24.com

The next day, we said our good-byes and were off down the empty road. I loved looking at the countryside; there was so much to look at. Mom entertained me with stories of her own childhood as we drove away. About three hours later, we arrived in Moscow, Idaho, at the university. There were people everywhere.

It was a crazy scene with parents helping their kids haul loads of stuff to the dorms. Suddenly, I felt weak, dizzy, and scared all at once. In less than a few hours, Mom would be leaving me here with all these strangers. I felt a wave of panic like never before go through me.

"Maggie, honey, isn't this exciting! You're about to have the best time of your life," Mom proudly announced. "It looks amazing, Mom! I can hardly wait to get started," I said with as much excitement I could muster.

We started moving my stuff into the dorms, along with the other new students and their parents. I would only be staying in the dorms for a week because I was going to join a sorority. Mom and Dad had both been in Greek fraternal living houses and had a blast, so I thought I would give it a shot as well. After stacking my stuff in a corner, Mom and I decided to meet up for lunch with a kid I knew while I was growing up. He was also a freshman at Idaho. Chris had lived across the creek from us; his mom, Jeanette, was like an aunt to me. Chris had come up to Idaho to play football. It was weird that we had known each from about three years old, and here we were going to college together. We were not close by any means, but it was nice to have him up there with me. At least I knew one person who could start off the school year with me.

Before I knew it, Mom was giving me a big hug and a kiss and was off down the road. I put on a brave face and turned toward the dorm to meet the roommate I'd be living with for rush week. During rush, we would go to a series of parties at all the sororities to find the right one for each of us. If a sorority picked you, and you picked them, it would be a match, and that sorority house would be where you were going to live. As I got back to my room, my roommate was moving her things in and saying good-bye to her parents. Her name was Beth. She was short, with long brown hair, was somewhat overweight, but had a charming look about her. After her parents left, we got to talk about almost everything. She was just as worried as I was about beginning college, which calmed my nerves a lot. Maybe this was how everybody started out a new adventure.

Getting ready for my senior prom (Courtesy the Hurst Family)

The view from Maggie's Mom "Maggie's Mom."

This has been my title for twelve years now. Yes, I have two other children and a husband. I am immensely proud of all three of them— and could write another story about them. Yes, I raise cattle and olives and am a painter. Yes, I cook and clean and keep a house. Yes, I am lots of other things; but mostly, when I am introduced to someone in our small community, I am known as Maggie's mom. At first I was proud, then scared, then embarrassed, then combative, and now proud again. This is my part of Maggie's story.

One of the first questions I am usually asked is if I noticed anything different about Maggie. Were there any signs in early childhood? The answer is honestly, "No." Then that leads to me wondering privately to myself: well, why not? Was I just blind? Was I really just a clueless, bad mom—blind to all the signs that there was trouble ahead? But no matter how hard I try to peck around in my memory, I simply can't find any early warnings. Amy, our oldest daughter, was a sunny, happy baby— my "starter" child. I had to learn all the baby, toddler, little girl lessons with her as my guinea pig. She was five when Maggie was born, and I remember making a concerted effort to make sure she didn't feel displaced by this squally new member of the family. Thomas, our son, was born two years after Maggie; so really, when I think about those years, I just remember diapers, dinners, cleaning, and more diapers. We were just a happy family finding our way together.

My husband, Joe, had started his own business in the hay, grain, and farm supply field. We moved to the country when Thomas was two, and then school occupied our lives for a long time. It seems as if there was always PTA, classroom parties, homework, youth soccer teams, Girl Scouts, and Cub Scouts (I even coached Thomas's little league team one year). I drove kids to school, from school to

games, to friends, to town; in fact, really all I did was to take care
of my kids for the twenty-five-plus years between 1970 when Amy
was born and 1996 when Thomas left for college. I served on the
Board of the Visiting Nurse Association, the local planning
commission, and ran the county farm bureau for seven years, but
mostly, I was just a mom.

Maggie was old for her grade. Her birthday fell in December, so
she couldn't start school until she was almost six. Then that next
year, we discovered that Amy, who was in the seventh grade, was
dyslexic. (When I finally got to see her records and asked why her
teachers had given her all As and Bs when she was having such
trouble reading, I was told she was such a good student and such a
joy to have in class that no one wanted to rock the boat!)

We took Amy to a special school in Los Angeles that summer for
an intensive program that promised to have her reading in two
months, and it worked. But they did tell us that we should probably
enroll her in a more structured program so that she would have to
continue to meet set goals—and not just be able to skate by on being
charming! Our only option was a local Christian school, and we
decided we might as well send both girls to the same school. Both
had to take an entry exam. While Amy passed just fine (though
they planned to start her reading in the fifth-grade level and then
move her up as soon as possible), Maggie didn't do so well. They told
us that they felt she should repeat kindergarten! I went back to ask
the teacher she had had for that year—a personal friend yet—and
the answer was the same: "Well, she was just such a joy to have in
class!" So I just chalked it up to a bad school, and we moved on. Both
girls did well in school, and Thomas started there too when he was
five. Amy was a great athlete in high school. She was a starter in
both basketball and softball, and I saw how much easier it was for
her to have friends and be involved when she was a teenager
because of her love of sports. Maggie and Thomas grew up going to

her games and sharing in her successes, so it was natural that they also got into sports big time once they were teenagers.

During Maggie's freshman year, her PE teacher asked her to turn out for the track team. Her grades were good, so we agreed, and she was off and running.

She started to run—and started to win—and just never looked back. It seemed that she won every race she entered. Her coach, Mr. Jim Roeber, became a trusted friend who took her under his wing.

She ran in increasingly important races, and her name began appearing in the local paper and then in regional papers, and then, it seemed all of a sudden, she was a star. Looking back now, I think she was already taking the first steps down the long road we have been traveling. I think when she was feeling down, she ran; the endorphins that were released into her system helped balance her brain, and the rush of winning must have kept the doubts away. Then when she was feeling too "up" (in her words, "kind of wired"), she would yell, "Going running, Mom." And two miles later, she would be tired and hungry and lay down for a good night's sleep, and all would be well again.

I also suspect that her running helped her brain in another way. Because she was an athlete, and so much was demanded of her body, I spent a lot of time making sure she ate the right food. We have always been an "eat dinner together at the table" family, so our meals were pretty structured. Now that I know so much more about bipolar kids, and how much what they put into their bodies can influence their mood, I think having me in charge of what she ate helped her to stay steady during her adolescent years—a time when so many bipolar kids start to go off track.

One last thing that helped her was her age. Because she was older than all of her classmates, I think it was easier for her to either be a leader or at least not have to try to fit in with her classmates. Most bipolar teens want so badly to feel better that they will try just about anything to achieve that end. Many things are tried; some work! Friends you can be better than, and alcohol that brings acceptance at parties, and drugs that somehow quiet the demons that are starting to talk to them. When you learn that three out of every one hundred teenagers are bipolar, then you realize that in your high school of 1,500 kids, there must be at least forty-five seriously ill kids who don't even have a clue that they are sick, and then you add in all the normally angst-ridden kids who are struggling to figure out who they are and where they fit in—well, no wonder high school can be such a mess! In her senior year, Maggie was heavily recruited by colleges all over the nation. I took her and three of her friends on a trip to visit colleges in Montana, Idaho, Washington, and Oregon. Looking back on that week, it was probably the last truly happy time that we would have for a long time.

Maggie decided on the University of Idaho. She liked the coach; he said she wouldn't have to be his star, that he would be happy if she ran fifth or sixth on the Vandal team. He told me that the department was very careful about keeping their athletes healthy, that they were a family, and that they only wanted to provide a good educational experience. Plus, Joe had graduated from the U of I and liked the idea of his daughter going back there. So the "home Chapter" of Maggie's life ended, and the exciting world of big-time athletics (that she was sure would lead her to the Olympics) began.

'Maggie is the superstar'- -JIM ROEBER, Sonora track coach

Sonora track star posts elite time in Mt. SAC meet

(Courtesy of Sonora Union Democrat)

SONORA TRACK

Hurst sets 3,200 mark

Hurst smashes two school records

Hurst, Morton make State

Hurst, Morton win titles

Athlete of the Week

Maggie has state in mind

STATE TRACK MEET

Morton, Hurst hit the big time

STATE TRACK

Hurst ends up in finals

University of Idaho freshman Maggie Hurst has taken over the No. 1 spot on the Vandal cross country team this fall.

Never too young to be No. 1

*This race was in San Diego where I placed third out of 120 elite college runners.
(Courtesy the Hurst Family)*

This race was in Montana where I placed in the top twenty. (Courtesy the Hurst family)

Chapter 2

IDAHO

In rush week, we were so busy I could hardly breathe. Besides the sorority activities, I had to fit in running practice and getting acquainted with my new cross-country team. It was overwhelming, and I could hardly grasp all that was going on. I called back home to tell everyone I was having a blast. But really, I felt sad and worn-out. I didn't understand how I could be feeling like this when I hadn't even gotten started. Rush is a series of parties for the freshman girls to attend to help you find "your house." I felt very lonely the entire week. It seemed to me that the girls were all wild party animals that just wanted to meet boys and get drunk. I guess there was nothing wrong with that, but it just was not in my agenda. My main concern was to do well at school and run like the wind! At the end of the week, I chose my sorority. I really liked the house, and the girls seemed really nice; there were also two girls who were on my track team.

My new sisters moved all my stuff into a small room that I shared with four other girls. I used this room mainly to store stuff in, change in, (maybe) study in, and hang out in if I wanted. But as for my new sleeping quarters—this was something I grew to hate with a passion. There were about one hundred bunk beds on the fourth floor, stacked so close together it made me feel claustrophobic.

It was very hard to get to sleep at night with so many bodies so close together. I was on a bottom bunk. The top bunk was about half an arm's length above me.

The first morning, I woke up and hit my head so hard on the top bunk, it made me dizzy.

We all ate together in a huge dining room. I am a picky eater, and the food was horrible, which made me miss Mom like no tomorrow. It was especially tough on me because I loved to eat. There were a lot of rules in the house to get used to, and I didn't like that either.

"Maggie, you are on bathroom-cleaning duty," one of my new sisters would say. "I know you don't like the chores, but everyone has to do them at some point," another added. So far, I didn't like much sorority life. I didn't feel that I fit in; the girls were all too much into drinking. Every night there was a party at a fraternity. There, girls would drink until they passed out or went home with some guy they didn't even know. The girls would invite me to "come out with us and live a little!" I would always give them one excuse or another. I didn't get into the drinking because of my running. After all, that was the whole reason I went to college—to run. I wanted to be an awesome runner, and to do that, I needed to stay focused.

Practice started a few days after rush. It was definitely another level than my old high school team, but I was expecting that. To get to know the team, and get in some good running before our first race, we went up to lake Coeur d'Alene. It was good to get away from the whole sorority scene and take a breath of fresh air. The girls on the team were all really nice and fun to be around.

My memories about camp now are just a blur. That is probably because what I learned there was a real shock. Out of the blue, one of my teammates took me aside and said, "Hey, Maggie, I just thought you should know, Sharon and the coach are an item." "What on earth are you talking about?" I whispered under my breath. "I caught them kissing," my teammate said.

It may not have been a big deal to a lot of people, but to me, it was devastating.

Why would our thirty-eight-year-old coach date a twenty-year-old coed on our team? He was an older man I looked up to, and he was having an affair with my teammate! Nobody on the team liked the situation, and I just knew that it would be trouble for the future. I had partly picked Idaho because I thought the coach was a good running coach and a good role model. Role model my foot! is all that I could think. What a massive distraction for our team, and the season hadn't even started! Needless to say, the rest of camp was horrible. I felt betrayed and wanted to go home.

Whatever good feelings I had left about starting college had been sucked out of me. It was as if I had a vacuum connected to my windpipe. I felt withdrawn and empty, but it was not only about the coach-teammate–love-affair fiasco, but about me as well. I began to experience a dull pain in my body and mind that was subtle, but always present. I kept thinking that whatever it was, it would go away in the next few days. I kept telling myself, Maggie, just pull yourself together.

School was hard to concentrate on, especially since everyone around me seemed so happy. Why couldn't I be like that? In my whole life, I had always been in control and knew where I had to go. Now I was clueless. I felt as if my mind was slowly unraveling and there was no stopping it.

I was like a ghost on campus, slipping silently between classes, clenching my jaw at the tension, and my body aching. I was overwhelmed by every assignment. Just getting all the books for my classes was enough to put me over the edge. The sorority was no better. I talked to no one. Girls asked if I was okay, and I gave them superficial answers like, "Oh yeah, I'm just trying to adjust to all the changes." I knew that it was more than just the changes though.

Erica and Sara from my team also lived in the sorority and did a lot to try to help me out. Though they tried, they could do nothing to get my spirits up. Deep inside my body and my mind, things were wrong, horribly wrong.

NOTE: Psychiatry teaches us that the body and mind are intimately linked, and the symptoms of one become the symptoms of the other. The GlaxoSmithKline Web site, bipolar.com, tells us that in mental states that involve both anxiety and depression, sufferers often experience bodily tensions—muscle cramps, upset stomach, headaches—that reflect their mental state. Often, physical exercise gives the body a chance to release the pent-up tension. For an athlete like Maggie, that kind of self-medication would be the natural resort.

Practice and races were the only things I enjoyed. I thought that if I ran extremely hard, I could lose these feelings of worthlessness. I stayed up with the top runners of the team. We ran fifty to sixty miles a week, worked out in the weight room, and did pool workouts. Angie, Sharon, and I were the top three runners of the team. We were always competing in our interval workouts, long runs, and gym workouts. Often, we would go to the gym and soak our lower bodies in ice water until we thought we might pass out from the cold. It was a painful thing to do, but it was good for preventing injuries. Angie was a junior, and Sharon a sophomore. Each had been the best runner as a freshman for Idaho. After practices, when I would go to the gym and soak in the ice water, I almost liked this physical pain because it made me forget the pain welling up inside me.

One time at the gym, Sharon startled me with an invitation to share in her secret world: "Hey, Mag, would you like to come to church with us?" I was shocked! I didn't know what to say. "Uh… yes," I stammered, still reeling. I didn't approve of her relationship with the coach, but in my secret world, I was lost and lonely.

So I went. "Maggie, I am so glad you could make it," Coach said. We were at the church, and he was side by side with Sharon. I was so disgusted by what they were involved in, yet here I was standing next to them. I should have told the coach to forget it and go find another school, but I was sick and needed company. While I regretted it, I would hang out with Sharon and Coach Brian a number of times over the season.

Mom and Dad flew up for my first race. Chuck Brewster, a family friend, also came. From Washington, Uncle Steve and Aunt Pat showed up. It was very comforting to have them all there. "Hey, Mags." Dad smiled. "Hey yourself," I said loudly. "How do you like college, hon?" Mom beamed. "It's just like you said, Mom, a blast so far," I lied.

Having my family and friends there did bring my spirits up a lot. For that, I ran a great race on the Moscow Golf Course. I came in first for our team, and third overall. Mom and Dad were so excited! I felt a brief moment of satisfaction, but the short high died down quickly. I put on a brave face for Mom and Dad. They thought I was just loving college and everything it had to offer.

I showed them my sorority, ate lunch with them, took pictures with Dad by his old SAE fraternity, and then, before I knew it, they were gone. Just like that, I had put on a big show, letting them think I was living the dream—excelling at school, making friends, loving my house, and running well. Oh, how I only wished that it were true.

Even though running was going well, my mental heath was declining. My first anxiety attack was in the basement of the house. I was sitting at one of the computers trying to do a paper for English. All of a sudden, I felt like I was going to die right there in the chair. My face became hot, sweat poured out of me, a massive pain grew in my chest, my heart was pounding much too fast, and my brain went into a complete panic mode. I wanted to scream for help to the other girls, but nothing came out. I just sat and stared at the screen, thinking I was about to die.

As the days passed by, I withdrew more and more, and it became very obvious. I would just stare out the windows with deep sadness growing in me.

The girls in the house tried to help, but it was hard for them to be supportive because I could not do my part: I couldn't reach out for help, not even a simple conversation. I felt hopelessness closing in on me. Even beyond that, the aches and pains that would penetrate my body day and night were really beginning to worry me. Food didn't taste good anymore, and it was difficult to sleep at night.

It was hard to get up in the morning; it was hard to take a shower. Heck! It was hard to brush my teeth! I kept thinking it would pass over soon, and I would again be Maggie the Star! But I was beginning to worry that I wouldn't live up to my own expectations.

Despite my depression, and all my doubts, my running career continued to soar and was the only thing that helped me keep my head up. I did really well in the Aztec Invitational at San Diego. I came in fifth out of about 200 runners, and first for my team. I beat out some UCLA girls, which was really exciting, and also got my first college medal. Mom, Dad, Chuck, Aunt Andra, Aunt Jan, and cousin Shelly came to the race to cheer me on. I didn't have much time to talk to Mom and Dad, so they didn't know there was anything wrong. During the trip, I had a tough time trying to be social with the team. I felt that I had nothing to say, which was strange for me. Only a year ago, I was always in the middle of every conversation. I kept telling myself to get it together.

From there, our team trained for our next big race in Montana. Mom and Dad didn't make that race. My old friend Jennifer from high school came (she was now living in Kalispell), and that was really special for me. Again, my race went well. I ran a personal best, placed in the top twenty in a massive field of runners, and came in first for my team again. Even so, the trip back to school in the vans seemed endless. The emptiness inside me was getting too big to handle. I couldn't even enjoy simple things, like watching the beautiful scenery.

I had my headphones on the entire ride back, so I didn't have to talk to any other team members.

Back at Moscow, there was a huge picture of me in the local paper and an article on how well I was doing. I just couldn't enjoy my success. Amazingly enough, I was still able to complete my schoolwork. I also made one friend at the house. Her name was Angie. Angie was a godsend. I don't know why she wanted to be my friend, but I loved it. She was a cute blonde with lots of spunk.

She told me I would feel better real soon. She told me that she also had a hard time adjusting to college as a freshman, but she was now a sophomore, and things were a lot better.

That was the first time I felt any hope for the semester. Angie had a truck that she took me everywhere in. We would meet each other for lunch and go to the mall to walk around and window-shop. She made me want to be my old self more than anything. I really fought the bad feelings off every day. I kept my head up, shook off the anxiety attacks, the worry that plagued me daily, the agitation, and even tried to ignore my loss of energy. Angie always had a smile on her face and made me want to be happy right there with her.

The next race was in Eugene, Oregon. Dad, Chuck, Grandpa, cousin Angie, and her husband, Tom, came. My mood was okay, but not great by any means.

I was very focused on running well. As I said, what kept me going was running well and my friendship with Angie back at the house. I came away from Eugene with another personal best and finished in the top twenty-five. That finish put my spirits up for the day, and it was good to see my family.

NOTE: According to bipolar.com, many sufferers of mental illnesses try to hide their affliction from others. They often have a feeling of letting others down because they are unable to cope with a situation— that is, even in the best of times, impossible to bring to a closure all by oneself. Even though sufferers often keep their real depression and anxiety a secret from loved ones, they depend heavily on the knowledge that those they love and care for really love and care for them. Family support—if even unknowing support—is crucial for the healing of those who suffer from depression, anxiety, and bipolar disorder.

Chapter 3

BROKEN

Disaster struck at a small race in Spokane. I remember that race so clearly as if it were yesterday. It was a November morning at a junior college. It was so cold I could see my breath. I felt good as far as my running ability was concerned, and had a good feeling I was going to win the race. It was a warm-up race for our big conference race in Salt Lake City the following week. I felt that if I could do well at Utah and go on to the nationals, maybe I could beat this junk going on inside me.

> **NOTE:** One of the weaknesses of self-medication, no matter how healthy the particular form a sufferer chooses may seem to be, is that without the knowing help of others, such self-medication may not actually be a cure. Then again, even if it were a cure, people in desperate straits tend to overdo it and push the cure to the point of its becoming a problem that only compounds the problem it was intended to cure. In Maggie's case, her self-medication (her running) was about to crash.

My sorority sisters drove up for the event, and my mom, Grandmother, and Chuck Brewster from home all showed up. Having all this support touched me very deeply. I wanted to run an awesome race, and I did just that. I went beyond even my own expectations. By the first mile, I was already leading by quite a distance as I passed my family and friends. When I passed them again with a mile to go, I started to feel a sharp stabbing pain in my right lower leg. I pressed on, trying to ignore the increasing pain. I figured I could overcome it and finish the race. The problem was that the pain intensified alarmingly with each step. I tried my best to ignore it, but it was killing me. It was so bad I was limping. My teammate Sharon started to gain on me as we headed into the last two hundred meters on the track. I couldn't let her win after I had run such a great race and endured all that pain in that last mile. I forced myself to sprint down the track with Sharon right beside me. As I ran toward the tape, I felt a sharp snap in my shin that was so painful I can't describe it even to this day. Even so, I muscled through the tape, winning the race by less than an inch. Then I fell to the side of the track holding my leg, with hot tears rolling down my cheeks. It was hard to breathe, and my skin was cold and clammy. I knew this was it. I had just ended my season. There would be no Utah, no Nationals, no Olympics. I had won the race, but I had lost running forever.

Mom knew immediately that I needed to go to the hospital, but my mind wasn't paying attention to what they were telling me. Instead, I felt myself drifting to another place. The main thing that had been holding me together had just been broken. I had won the race but ended my running career; in my mind at the time, it was definite and overwhelming. I just knew there was no coming back. I was sure, beyond any doubt, that it was all over for me. I was lost in a vast sea of despair, and yet, in a strange kind of way, I couldn't admit it either.

We got back to Idaho, and Coach said I probably just sprained something—and they would wrap it. My mom said "no way" and took me to the local hospital.

At the hospital, the x-rays showed a jagged fracture all the way up my shinbone. I didn't want to believe anything the doctor told us. I felt sick when the doctor said, "Well, Maggie, you will have to be in a full leg cast, you will have to have crutches, and you may not be able to do any running until spring, or maybe longer—depending on how well your leg heals." It was a sad, lonely drive back to school, even though Mom was with me. I felt my body finally give in to the sadness that I so vigorously had tried to fight off. There was no escaping my own crying, or the pain in my chest, or the worry, or the anxiety.

Back on campus, things only became worse. I had to go everywhere on crutches. Angie tried her best to help me, but I just couldn't hold my spirits up anymore, which drained her a lot. I lost my appetite, my silky blonde hair that I had been so proud of became dull and limp, my skin broke out with acne everywhere, and my body became weaker and weaker. The weather brought more heartache, with tons of snow and ice, and the temperature dropped below zero degrees Fahrenheit. I would just lie on my bunk bed and let the tears flow steadily. The only thing I thought about was death. I thought of it as a way out of the pain that was stabbing me every moment of those endless days. I knew definitely that there was something very seriously wrong with me. Who thinks about dying all day and just cries for no reason? This sort of thing had never happened to me before. I had always loved my life; I used to thrive on meeting people, learning new things, and just being me! Now I barely felt alive. I started calling Mom three to four times a day in a panic. I told her I was sad and wanted to come home.

My mother tried her best to encourage me; she said, "Maggie, honey, I know you're going to be okay. You're feeling bad about your leg and having some homesickness. That is totally normal. I know you will come out of this real soon. Just hang in there, sweetie." It was hard not to worry her, but I felt if I didn't tell somebody how I was feeling, I really might die. I felt nonstop sadness and worthlessness all day and all night. It felt as though somebody was constantly twisting a large knife in my stomach. Angie and the rest of my sorority sisters were always asking if I were all right. I always answered that I was fine and my leg was just sore. I know they probably thought I was some weirdo. I never went to social functions, meetings, or even dinner. I would just lie in bed longer and longer each day.

Chapter 4

THANKSGIVING

Just before I left Idaho for Thanksgiving vacation, I heard some really bad news. Brian resigned as head coach for cross-country and track and field. His romance with Sharon had turned into a serious scandal. The rumor was that the school would fire him if he didn't resign. Thanksgiving vacation came, and I flew home for a week. Mom and Dad could barely recognize me. I was underweight, my hair was short, my skin had turned pale, and my usually ever present smile was nowhere to be seen. Mom really started to worry when she saw me. She took me to Dr. M. for a checkup. He had always been our family doctor, and though I had known him for a long time, I just stared at the wall while he asked questions about my health and what I was eating and how I was getting along at college.

"Maggie, I see that your body fat is below 6 percent," he said. "Have you lost your menstrual cycle?" I told him I had. He also noted that my iron count was extremely low and said that was probably why I was anemic. I barely listened to him. He didn't pick up on my depression but did prescribe me some iron and vitamins.

Being home for that week was unsettling in so many ways. I now lived at a college, and what I had called home my entire life was now just a place to visit.

Before I left for college, I cleaned out my room so that Mom could use it as a guest room. My sister had done that when she left for college, and it worked out well. Now, though, for me it was a major change.

For instance, nothing about my room felt familiar. I had always loved my room. Yes, it still had flowered wallpaper, and a beautiful view of the creek below, and bull pines out one window, and aspen trees out the other—which were all still there. But there were none of my posters, none of my medals thumbtacked on the walls, none of my trophies standing here and there, none of my clothes in the closet—they were all gone! My room didn't feel like my room; it felt cold and empty. I felt sad and hollow inside.

I decided to take a bath. As I stood in front of the bathroom mirror, I hardly recognized myself. I actually looked frail, with cyst like inflammations all over my shoulders and back, and my hair had turned dirty blonde and felt coarse. I was horrified, but I started the bath and tried not to think of the past, without much success. This time the previous year, I had just finished running in the top twenty of state meet for cross-country, and I had a boyfriend that I thought I was in love with. I also felt very self-confident, and everyone said I looked great. Not anymore! As I soaked in the bath, I sank down under the water until I couldn't hold my breath any longer and came up for air. I imagined what it would be like to drown. That scared me, and I jumped out of the tub and dried off. Why was I thinking awful thoughts all the time? I couldn't figure it out, but I sure didn't want to tell my family either. I wanted to get better all by myself and just move on.

But even at the familiar old dinner table, I felt like an alien. Dinner at the Hurst house had always included laughter, good ranch-style cooking, great conversation, and lots of personal warmth. All I felt was emptiness. There was a bright spot toward the end of the week though.

I had always been very proud of my brother, Tom, and he was getting ready for his big cross-country state meet at Fresno. I went to see him run. Tom ran like the wind, and his team did great too.

Something else happened at my brother's meet. I had been thinking of leaving Idaho because of the coaching scandal, and suddenly, at trackside in Fresno, I met the head coach for Cal Poly, San Luis Obispo. When I told the coach who I was and that I was thinking about transferring, I immediately had her interest. I could tell she had been very impressed with my freshman cross-country season. She took down all my information, and I told her I would be calling her. I thought that if I went somewhere else for school, my mood would improve—and I could leave behind Idaho's freezing weather.

Back home, I announced the good news. "Mom, I talked to the Cal Poly coach at Tom's race." I felt a bit uncomfortable because I knew it would sound like I was acting on a whim. I was right. Mom sounded a little worried. "Mags, hon, don't you think it's just a bit hasty to switch schools so soon after only one semester?" she said.

I just had to get the point across. "Mom, there is no longer a coach at Idaho.

Why should I go there? I don't really have any friends, I don't like the cold, and I don't fit in being in the sorority at all," I whined. She replied, "Mags, I am just worried you're making decisions based on being in a down place because of your leg." That hit me hard, and my mood swung, and though I tried not to show it, I just wanted to scream to her and say, "It's not my leg! There is something wrong with me! I just want to crawl underground and die!" But I didn't say any of that. I just smiled and said, "Let's see how things go, okay, Mom?"

> **NOTE:** Stress in general can affect a person's physical appearance and health. It is quite possible that the stress Maggie was experiencing was at least an aggravating factor in the cystic acne she noticed on her back while preparing to shower, according to information gleaned from the article "Psychodermatology: The Mind and Skin," by John Koo, MD, and Andrew Lebwohl, in The American Family Physician for December 1, 2001, and further information obtained from the Web site quickcare.com.

Maggie's Mom

At college, things started to go wrong right from the beginning. The coach was about 180 degrees from what he had told us! He ran Maggie to death—sixty miles a week—and they scheduled practices exactly during her mealtimes, so she often got back to her sorority and had to scrounge for sandwiches. The races started, and she was running faster than ever, but not enjoying it much anymore. She started to have trouble focusing on her classes. She discovered the coach was having a romantic relationship with a girl on the team. She found a few friends at the sorority, but they seemed to do a lot of partying and drinking, which made her like an outsider for the first time in her life. She sent me a picture that was in the local paper, all about her amazing success as a freshman on the team;

and while I was thrilled with the story, I didn't like the picture at all! There was something wrong with her eyes.

And then the phone calls started—at first once a day, and later, sometimes three or four times a day. At first, she just seemed to need reassurance, but later, I found myself grasping for ideas to help her just get through the afternoon. I finally decided I needed to go up there and see for myself. I made arrangements to fly to Spokane, meet my mother, and go to Maggie's next race. We got to the track meet just ahead of the van from the school, and when the doors opened up and the team got out, I didn't recognize her for a minute. Her hair was still long and blonde—and her eyes were still blue—but her body looked odd. She seemed flat and out of focus. I was shocked and remember telling my mom that something was really wrong.

There is a lot of hoopla at a big college cross-country race. There is a long start, and then the runners all disappear and show up again at the end. If you check out the course, however, you can usually hurry to a place along the circuit where you can watch them come by. I rushed over to what I thought would be about midway. When the first runner came out of the trees, I was thrilled to see it was my Maggie! Then she got closer and closer and passed me with such a driven look on her face that when I realized that the next runners were probably two hundred yards back, I felt panic. Something was wrong; she was a great runner, but she shouldn't be this far out in front at this point in the race! So I went back to await the big finish, which is usually down the straightaway in front of the bleachers. The cheering started. I leaned forward to watch, and she came out first, but just barely first—the rest of the pack had caught up to her.

Then I realized something was really, really wrong. She was laboring, limping, lunging—it was awful to watch. It was like watching a racehorse break down on the track: people around me were gasping; my mother was hanging on to my arm crying; and in front of us, she somehow lurched across the finish line—still in front, but by just one step! When we picked her up off the track, she said she had fallen just before entering the stadium. I told the coach that I would take her back to the campus.

He took us to a student athlete emergency room on the campus. The attendants said they thought she had a bad sprain, and they planned out a program so she could start physical therapy right away, but it might be a while before she could run again. Something didn't seem right, so I called Joe, and he told me to take her into an emergency room in town and to insist on an x-ray. When I told the coach that was what I was going to do, he told me that the university didn't operate that way, that they needed to depend on their own medical diagnoses, and that if we went off campus, we would have to pay for it. I said okay and went anyway. The x-ray showed a spiral fracture of her left shinbone. She had finished the last one hundred yards on a broken leg! They put a cast on her leg, and the coach seemed apologetic for his mistaken diagnosis. The girls in the sorority were solicitous and kind to Maggie in my presence. The college officials assured us that the "full ride" was still in effect—they would not renege on her scholarship. Maggie was quiet, but also seemed relieved. I remember wondering if the stress she had been under was just too much and maybe this was a blessing in disguise. She would be in the cast for six weeks, then in physical therapy until spring, and would have plenty of time to get ready for the next track season. In the meantime, she could concentrate on classes and just being a regular girl. Since she would be home for Thanksgiving in just two weeks, I left her there and flew home, trying to tell myself that everything would be fine.

Within two days, the phone calls started again. This time, she seemed totally desperate—not even rational—and each time I would beg her to just hang on one more day, that tomorrow things would be better, and that she would be home in just a few days, and then we could talk face-to-face and figure out what to do.

At Thanksgiving, she came home, and I took her to our family doctor. He talked to her for quite a while and x-rayed her leg. He came into the waiting room and told me that while her leg was healing well, he felt she was depressed and needed some medication. He said he thought she was having a rough time adjusting to life as a non-runner. He felt that running had defined her life for so long that she was just left at loose ends. I asked him if he thought she should go back to school. He said he thought so, but to just wait and see how she felt. I don't even remember what medication he gave her (that's how unimportant I thought it was).

Joe and I talked it over; it was only three weeks between Thanksgiving and Christmas vacation, so we agreed to her request, and off she went again. This time, she had a good week and a half before the phone began to ring again.

Tears, sobs, loneliness—I don't know how I convinced her every day that she would be okay and that she needed to go down to the sorority kitchen and make a cup of tea; and that she could go to the library and read a magazine; and that she could go to the counseling office, and they would find someone for her to talk to; and that it would only be three more days until the weekend, then just two; and that if she could just last until the vacation and then didn't want to go back to school, that would be fine; and that we could talk when she got home.

Amy called and said she had a flight to Spokane and would go see Maggie. I was relieved because I thought it would get her through a few more days.

By the time her Christmas vacation came, Joe and I decided that we would move her home even if it was temporary. It just wasn't worth the worry and pain, and we needed to face the fact that

Idaho was over! When we did get home, it was such a relief—mostly because the phone was not ringing for me.

We had a worried Christmas, a worried, quiet Christmas with lots of talking, lots of discussion about what she could do if she decided not to go back. We spoke of how we could just take some time and maybe enroll her in the local junior college. (I was still going with the explanation that she was just trying to get used to not running for the time being. The idea that there could be anything seriously wrong just was not on the radar; she just needed to decide to change directions, and be and do something else for a while!) I ran into a friend of mine, Donna Reese, whose boys had gone to school with Maggie. She told me she had heard about Maggie's broken leg. She said her own older son had just dropped the bombshell that he wasn't happy in college either, and they were wondering what that would mean. We commiserated a bit and then went our separate ways. I often think about the consequences of that meeting. Donna is a very religious person while I wasn't at all. She told me she would pray for Maggie; I thanked her but really didn't think anymore about it.

Now, all these years later, I wonder if it was her prayer that brought Maggie to God's ear. They say He works in mysterious ways, and the "ways" that were in front of us were certainly mysterious.

Donna and Jim Reese (Courtesy the Reese family)

Chapter 5

MOSCOW

Flying back to Idaho after Thanksgiving was like a bad dream. I just wanted to jump out of that plane and be permanently rid of the despair that controlled me.

As we were coming in for the landing in Moscow, I felt as if I was descending into an ice world of doom.

I was always cold in the sorority, always cold even in the heated classrooms; it seemed that everything was cold, cold, cold. My world was one big ice block.

Everywhere I went was punishing. I constantly slipped with my crutches and the big boot cast.

I started calling my sister every chance I could get her. "Amy, I feel like I am dying," I would tell her. Amy tried to cheer me up: "Maggie, I know you're going to get through this. I went through some lonely times in college, and it will pass." My standard reply was "I know I am not going to make it, Amy, I just know it." Amy was worried by these phone calls, and she called Mom and Dad to voice her concerns about me. They were still trying to keep a positive outlook on my situation and told Amy that I would get through this. Even my sister started calling me to try to cheer me up. One wonderful day, she said, "Mag, I am going to fly up to Spokane, and I'll come get you for the weekend, okay?" I agreed, even though I had no energy and knew I wouldn't be any fun; but oh, it was wonderful that she was coming! When I think back to that day, I realize that Amy was so caring, flying all the way to Spokane, then driving two hours to Moscow, then picking me up, and driving all the way back to Spokane. Plus, she paid for everything. "Mags, it's so good to see you," she said with a big smile. All I could think of to say was "Thanks for coming all this way, Amy, I really appreciate it." We stayed at a hotel in Spokane. It was snowy everywhere, which made me feel even worse.

I found that it was even hard to be around my sister. I felt like I was dragging her down with me. I just wanted so badly to curl up in a ball and sleep. My depression had gotten to the point where I didn't even want to get through the day.

On our way to dinner, we stopped in the middle of a beautiful snowy bridge to look down at the icy Spokane River below. A horrible image pervaded all my thoughts; I imagined diving into that river. In shock, I demanded, "Amy, let's get off this bridge now." I was really starting to scare myself with thoughts like these. My sister could sense something was wrong and tried to comfort me.

"Maggie, I know you don't feel too good now, but it will pass, and you'll feel good again, I promise," she persisted.

I didn't really believe her. That night, I tossed and turned in bed, wishing desperately that these feelings of hopelessness would leave me. It's an awful thing to think about ending your life—especially as I had loved my life so much.

I was filled with fear and confusion. There were only fixable things wrong in my life—why was I having thoughts of ending it? This was so perplexing to me, nothing made sense anymore, and my mind could not rest. There was no escaping my nightmares. I became more and more irritated, confused, and frustrated with each passing day.

The last few days of the semester at Idaho were barely survivable in my mind. By then, I told Coach I was leaving school at the semester and transferring to Cal Poly, San Luis Obispo. I didn't care how he felt about it either. I felt that he had given up on our team for a relationship with my teammate. There would be no nationals, no championships, and no future for running at Idaho. I just wanted to scream at him that I was in so much pain, and he hadn't made it any easier. He didn't even seem to care.

My parents showed up at the end of the semester to move me out. I was leaving for good, giving up a hard-earned full-ride scholarship and my dreams of running in the NCAA Nationals. I said good-bye to hardly anyone. The ride home seemed endless. Everywhere I looked seemed bleak and dark; everything I saw outside mirrored what I felt on the inside. I felt responsible for everything; I felt that I had failed my parents, had failed Idaho, and had failed my hometown of Jamestown and all the people there who had supported me in my running career.

Maggie, just be happy and get over it, I told myself. I couldn't though; I couldn't even fake a smile for anyone.

Amy's View

My little sister was at the top of her game! She had a full-ride scholarship to a great school, she was beautiful, she was going places! I was not only proud of her, but I was also just a little bit jealous. I was five years older than Mags, so my life was headed in a different direction, but I still tried to stay in touch by phone. In fact, it was on the phone that I began to realize that something wasn't quite right. She sounded very sad and lonely. I tried to offer advice and support and tell stories of my college experiences to let her know it was tough for me to go away from home. Then she broke her leg, and the phone calls changed.

She started to call me all the time, almost every day. I finally decided that perhaps I could go and visit. I am a flight attendant for a major airline, so I flew to Spokane, rented a car, and drove to Moscow. When I arrived, it seemed like there were fires to put out everywhere! She was having problems with the girls in the sorority, but when I met them, they seemed interesting and nice. Maggie hated the food, so we figured out snack and food options. I even went up to the sleeping porch to set up her bed better so she could sleep easier. Finally, I decided to take her back to Spokane for a weekend. I tried to stay upbeat and positive, but the person before me was scared, lonely, and unsure. I didn't know what was going on—and I didn't know what to do—and I didn't know my sister at all.

Amy, our brother Tom, and me. (Courtesy the Hurst family)

Chapter 6

SAN LUIS OBISPO

Once again, when we arrived at the ranch, it was not the happy place for me that it once was. I found no comfort even in my favorite cat, Matilda. She would jump up on my bed and burrow herself into the covers next to my head and purr.

Me and Matilda the cat in the midst of my depression in 1996.

(Courtesy the Hurst family)

It was as if she knew I was in a deep sadness. Even Mom's food seemed bland.

I had always loved Mom's cooking; now I didn't even want to eat. I had lost my sense of things and all my happiness.

After about a week, I convinced Mom and Dad that I could go to Cal Poly, San Luis Obispo, and make it work. The running coach got me in, and I signed up for fifteen units of classes as well as the athletics program. That New Year's Eve was a tough one. I packed up my things, and Mom and I were set to go traveling once again. Though I could hear fireworks and people celebrating, I was deeply depressed for no obvious reason. When we set off the next morning, I wanted to tell Mom to just stop and turn around. I knew I did not have the strength to pull it off.

After she helped me move in at Cal Poly, Mom looked worried as she pulled away from the curb. I was as scared as I had ever been in my life. The minute I lost sight of Mom, I had an anxiety attack. It felt like I was going to die right on that curb. My heart was racing, sweat was pouring down my face, and my breathing was so rapid it felt like I couldn't get a breath. After I regained myself and found that I was actually still alive, I slowly trudged back to my dorm.

At the dorm, everyone seemed to know each other. After all, it was now their second semester. I felt very alone, even more so than at Idaho. That first day, I willed myself to stay away from the phone. I wanted so badly to call Dad and have him come get me. I just wanted those awful feelings to go away.

The next morning, classes began. I was overwhelmed by having new professors, new fellow students, and homework, which was assigned to us right away. I was in a full state of panic. I would leave each class early and just wander around campus trying to calm myself down. What was happening to me? When it came time to eat at the cafeteria, I would skip the meal and go to my room. I was at Cal Poly for a week and was getting worse with each day. By Saturday, I was in a state of panic. I called Dad at work and told him to come and get me right away. I pleaded, "Dad, I just need to rest, please, I just can't stay here." He was shocked by the tone of my voice and left work immediately and drove the six hours to Cal Poly without stopping. When he arrived, he packed my stuff into the truck and took me back home.

Maggie's Mom - Home Again

We settled into an uneasy coexistence after Christmas. Then the athletic director at San Luis Obispo called Maggie. He had heard that she was home and offered her a complete scholarship to come down and run for them. No pressure, lots of rehab, tutors, and whatever she needed. Just come! Now Joe and I were both against it, but Maggie overrode every objection, and she and I were on the road again; and sure enough, a few days later, Joe had to bring her home. This time, there was finality to the whole thing. College was not the answer, and we would try another direction.

Chapter 7

DESPERATE

Though I was back at home, I was a basket case. Mom was trying everything she knew to make me happy again. After a few days of crying all day, I got a call from Angie, my sorority sister at Idaho. She said, "Mags, you just got to come back. We all miss you so much. I know we can make things work up here for you. I just know it. Come on, Mag, please!" After her phone call, I thought maybe she was right. Maybe I could make everything work after all. I could go back and fix everything that I had abandoned. I could make it right again. Mom was against that plan, and Dad did not agree at all and said I should wait the semester out and work on getting my strength up. Against their wishes, I packed just my clothes into a few suitcases and headed north to what turned out to be a desperate, dark, and lonely place.

I had hoped that my three weeks away was enough to make it work again in Moscow. I should have listened to Dad and stayed home.

As I walked into the sorority house, I knew I had made an extremely bad mistake. I went upstairs and started unpacking my things. I immediately burst into tears. I tried to stop but couldn't. My sobs got louder and deeper.

"Maggie, you're going to be okay. Trust me," Angie said. "No, my life is over. I just want to go home and sleep. I need my mom and dad," I wailed. Some other girls came in to comfort me, but I just waved them away. I went to class, but just stared into space. I could feel myself slipping more and more into an abyss I could not escape. For two days, I just wandered around the campus, hardly talking with anyone, not sleeping, eating hardly at all, and staring into the abyss. It all came to a head when I began to have thoughts of wandering into a snowstorm and freezing to death. I couldn't get these horrible images out of my head. I called Dad and cried, "I feel like I am going to die. I can't go to school anymore. You were right. I made a mistake by coming back here. Please come get me!"

My poor father. Just a month ago, he drove all the way to Idaho to move me out of there. Two weeks ago, he came down to San Luis Obispo to rescue me. And now, I needed him to get me out of Idaho again. Dad doesn't fly. He actually hates the idea of traveling by airplane. But after my call, he was on a plane in two hours. (I was told it took a lot for him to get on the plane.) When Dad arrived, he gathered me into the rental car and took me over to a Travelodge motel to decide what to do next. He could tell I was in terrible shape and figured he would talk to the school's doctor. The doctor told my father it was not worth the risk to my health for me to try toughing it out for the remainder of the semester. He suggested taking me home and getting me to see a doctor and a counselor. So Dad did just that. We packed my things in boxes and took them to the post office to ship home. After that, we jumped in the car and headed for the airport. I was so upset that I don't remember the trip home.

Amy's View - A Flying Trip with My Dad

One day after Christmas, I got a frantic phone call from my dad. He had just talked to Maggie and was afraid for her. There had been a major winter storm in the Pacific Northwest, and he didn't think he could make the drive to pick her up in time. I asked, "In time for what?" "She wants to die, Amy," my dad said frantically. "I have to get up there now!" One of the perks of my job is free travel, and at that time, free travel for my parents. My dad had never taken me up on my offers because he hated to fly. I checked on the loads, and they were great, plus I had the day off—so I told him I would meet him at the gate. I have flown now for fifteen years and have never had a passenger like my dad that day. During the entire two-hour flight, he gripped the armrests. His face was bright red, he was hunched over, and half the time, his head was between his knees. He wouldn't talk; but since flying was not an ordeal before his tour of Vietnam, I suspected that he was having flashbacks to the TET offensive in 1967. I served him Bloody Marys and just tried to be reassuring. I saw such dedication in my father that day. He was tackling an impossibly large fear to take care of his family.

Chapter 8

DESPAIR

I felt so ashamed as I walked in the door to my parents' home. Mom came over and hugged me and told me that we would make it through whatever was going on. When I went up to my room to rest, it seemed even like less of a place of comfort than it had ever seemed before. The flowers on the wallpaper had always seemed happy and alive, but now they were dead and colorless. It took me forever to put my clothing away. I felt like every part of my body was a massive weight. I had never felt so lost and alone.

Mom had set up two appointments for the next day. One appointment was with our doctor, and the other was with a counselor. The doctor diagnosed me with depression. He did not know how long it would be until I'd get over it.

He immediately started me on an antidepressant called Zoloft. He said that we would increase the dose gradually. While I was relieved that there was a name for what was wrong with me, I was also very frustrated because I didn't know how long this depression would last. I just wanted my life back! I wanted my smile back! Was that too much to ask? Then I went to see my new counselor.

Her name was Kate, and she was wonderful. During our first appointment, we talked about what I experienced when I began to feel sad, and discussed some ways to get through the sad days.

As time went on back at home, my days seemed endless. I would lie on my bed and just stare at the flowers on the walls with tears streaming down my face.

The only relief I had was falling asleep. Mom would bring up food and drink throughout the day. Instead of skipping meals, as I had done at Idaho, I had started eating all day long. I went from 115 pounds to 150 pounds, seemingly overnight! When I looked in the mirror, I had changed even more. My skin was covered with acne, and those cysts on my back had not gone away; my eyes were dull and had dark circles under them, and my hair was even worse than it had been.

Amy's View - At Home

For the next three months, our lives were upside down. I tried to come home every chance I was off to help. My parents were exhausted. My brother was finishing his senior year at high school and just trying to stay out of the way! My sister was gone, just a shell was left behind. We were all afraid to leave her alone. Voices were raised. I remember, one day, my dad—also a health food aficionado—came home with a whole armful of carrots and announced that he had just read that if Maggie just ate more carrots, she would be better. My mom actually burst into tears, ran into their bedroom, and slammed the door!

Chapter 9

DINNERTIME

Night after night, dinner was painful for the entire family. Dad would try to start light conversation, but nobody was really interested as they were all worried about me. I hated that feeling: the knowledge that my condition was the source of their pain. I didn't talk at all; I just stared down at my plate and ate.

After dinner, I curled up and watched television. My one happy moment of the day was watching my favorite sitcom, Seinfeld, but even as I watched it, I pulled out my hair strand by strand. My mom made me sit on my hands so I wouldn't pull it all out. As for cleaning myself, it was a massive chore. I would take a bath and just sit there and cry. While in the bath, I would think about drowning myself. That is why I hated bath time.

The worst night of my depression was the night I told my family I wanted to die. We were all sitting at the dinner table, and I just broke down crying. "Just let me die," I sobbed. My father started sobbing. It was the most awful thing for me to see Dad cry. I felt so guilty, but there was nothing I could do. Mom was the strong one that night and just held my father. The very next day, Mom decided we needed a road trip. We drove all the way to Palm Springs to see my grandma. Mom and I stopped along the way to see Joshua Tree National Park. I was so amazed at the way Mom didn't get depressed by my horrible mood. She always was pointing things out and talking about what a great adventure we were having. Seeing my grandma was really a needed lift. She treated me as if nothing were out of the ordinary. It was a welcome break from lying in my room all day long. I started to feel a tiny bit better.

Chapter 10

OUT OF DARKNESS

Even after we returned home, I continued to feel better. After a month on Zoloft, and then a change to a new medication, I began to feel better somehow.

I found that the things I had felt were difficult were now easy. I even began to look for a job. I applied for an ice cream–vendor job in Yosemite National Park.

Kate, my counselor, suggested I start a journal to try to make sense of my life.

Journal Entry - March 16, 1996

I finally have some good news! I got the job in Yosemite National Park. I start in April. I am a little nervous about leaving home, but I feel it is a step in the right direction as far as my road to recovery. I have also applied at the Fashion Institute in San Francisco. I thought it might be a different route for me to go instead of college. Tom continues to do well in his senior year in track and field. Today he won all his races at the Redskin Invitational. I was so proud of him.

Amy has been doing very well in her new job as a flight attendant.

She works for United Airlines. It is so great not to feel so depressed lately. I guess this medicine is taking effect. I have to start on a portfolio for the fashion school. It is located right in downtown San Francisco. I am really excited about doing something so different.

Right now, I feel so thankful for such a caring family. I think we have all weathered the storm. Matilda and I are off to sleep.

Journal Entry - March 24, 1996

I made it into the fashion institute! I am really proud of myself about getting in. I did a really cool project that was full of color and purpose. I dressed up in a Benetton suit and went to a thirty-minute interview. It was so fun to walk with Mom in the city with the cool breeze on my face. I finally felt alive for the first time in seven months. When I start school in San Francisco, I might live with Amy.

It is great to finally start making progress.

Journal Entry - March 27, 1996

Today I did lots of laundry with Mom. It was nice to do a small chore and not feel burdened. We also had a nice lunch together. I don't think Mom will ever know how much I appreciated all the time she spent with me these past three months. I mean, what kind of mom brushes your hair, feeds you anything you want to get a smile, and takes you on a spur-of-the-moment trip? An amazing mom does.

My room is a terrible mess right now, but it feels like too much of a burden to pick it up. I know I am getting better, but things still are sometimes overwhelming. The worst thing about being home again is being alone. All my friends are gone, and college seems like a distant memory. As for my running career, I think it is done forever.

When I think about running, that's what devastates me the most. I was just getting to be good. I just know I was going to be big. I had confidence, the talent, and the belief that I could be the champion. I had this dream that I was going to run for Nike and do these awesome commercials with my long blonde hair flowing in the breeze. Now the dream has faded away like a distant memory.

Journal Entry - March 30, 1996

It is 9:45 in the evening, and everybody is asleep. These are the times I feel very lonely. It feels like my heart might break into pieces.

I called all my old friends from high school, but nobody was home.

I then got out my scrapbooks to remember all the good times. That just made me feel worse. When I looked through the pictures, I saw the healthy, happy Maggie Hurst, and that was tough to see. Would I be okay at my new job in Yosemite? Please, God, just let me be normal. I will do anything to have me be all right. I will do my best to make this new plan work. I cannot let my parents down. Nobody understands why all this crap has happened. Sometimes I just feel like a frightened animal that is lost. No one did anything to hurt me in any way, nothing brought on this lousy depression, except maybe my shattered leg. For now, I have my wonderful soft velvety cat Matilda to purr against me all night. Tomorrow, Mom, Dad, and I are off to Yosemite. I hope everything goes all right.

NOTE: Medications can vastly improve a depression sufferer's outlook and provide a window that reminds the patient what normalcy feels like and can give hope for the future. However, in treating depression, doctors have found that the success is often temporary and that adjustments in treatment often have to be made. The road to recovery is full of unexpected twists and turns. It is important to keep in mind that while those who suffer depression (or mania as the case may be) may experience times of hopelessness, sheer persistence on the part of loved ones and family, medical personnel, and especially on the part of the person undergoing treatment is the most powerful source of hope. Sometimes, ironically and unpredictably, the antidepressant meant to end depression can trigger the opposite pole of behavior—mania—in a person who has a latent tendency toward bipolar disorder. (Information gleaned from mayoclinic.com and bipolar.com.)

Chapter 11

YOSEMITE

Going to Yosemite was worrisome and unsettling. I had so much anxiety in me; I felt as though I would burst at the seams. I would be living up there for the summer and working the ice cream stand. It seems simple enough, but for me, it was a terrifying challenge. As I packed my things into the tent cabin that I was assigned to, I couldn't help but worry that I was going to freak out again, get kicked out, and get picked up, and moved home again.

Mom and Dad gave me big hugs and lots of assurance that everything would be fine. After they left, a calm feeling filled me. As I was putting my stuff away, my new roommate walked through the door. She was about 5'3", had pretty long brown hair, with dark brown eyes, and a big smile. I knew instantly that she was a kind person; I could just tell by the way she carried herself. Her name was Beth. Later that evening, we ate dinner together and talked easily about everything. Maybe Yosemite would be my saving grace after all.

In the days that followed, I began to feel better with each passing moment.

I guess the new meds were really taking effect. I was so busy with my new job and making new friends, I barely had time to call my parents. I think they liked the break too. It meant that I was on my way to a full recovery. I worked six hours a day at an ice cream shop called Happy Isles. Then in the evening, I served pizza. When I did have time off, I would hike around the valley floor with Beth or other friends I had met. Talking to people was so easy now. I was actually happy again! As I think back, the next three weeks were a blur. Everything I did was fast-paced. I found that I could not slow down to relax. First, I would work all day, then change my clothes, then run over to a friend's cabin to see if they wanted to go have fun. If they didn't, I would charge off by myself and explore.

Yosemite was fascinating in every way imaginable, and I had so much energy, I had to release it somehow. One day after work, I got the wild idea that I should just run all the way up to the top of Vernal Falls along the Mist Trail, even though that trail was very steep, wet, and dangerous to run on. I started pulling stunts like this daily because of this newly found, incredible energy. I began to feel like I could do anything I wanted and nobody could stop me or tell me that it wasn't possible. I called home and told my parents that I needed a car up there so I could come home and visit. They didn't see anything wrong with the idea, and soon I had a car. Now I had a way of expanding my adventures and fun. I decided that I would take a couple of my new friends and show them my parents' place.

Chapter 12

WARNINGS

That trip to the ranch was the first time since I began feeling better that I thought that perhaps I was going out of control in a new direction. On the ride home, I rode the brakes most of the way down the mountain, and near the bottom, the brakes seemed to go out, but I thought it was exhilarating! When I told Mom and Dad what happened, they were worried once again—not only about the car, but also about the "friends" I brought home. These friends were not like my nice tent cabin mate Beth, but immediately struck Mom and Dad as disreputable, probably dishonest, and definitely untrustworthy people. That I had mistaken these people to be acceptable friends suggested that I was off track again! Poor Mom and Dad might have suspected I was in trouble, but had no idea I was headed for even bigger and deeper trouble. After our brief visit, my "friends" and I drove into Sonora, and I bought a pair of Rollerblades and some workout clothes. I thought that rollerblading would be a good way to get back in shape. After we had come back up over the mountains and were headed downslope toward the Yosemite Valley floor, I was overcome with an overwhelming desire to do something really crazy. I thought it would be fun to drive right on the edge of the road and look down into the depths of the valley just to make the drive exciting.

By the time we got back to Yosemite, it was evening. My "friends" jumped out of the car almost while it was still moving and told me they never wanted to go anywhere with me again. Their comments didn't faze me; I was ready for my next adventure. My dangerous driving was fun as far as I was concerned.

That night, I couldn't sleep at all, so at three in the morning, I tried out my Rollerblades, skating down the trails with only the full moon for light. It was amazing to be out so late and by myself and having so much fun skating.

I had the next day off from work, and my sister was coming up to visit me (and, I'm sure, to check up on me after my latest, and very odd, visit home)

NOTE: The Mayo Clinic Web site, which details both ends of the bipolar spectrum, tells us that the common symptoms of mania in patients include euphoria, extreme optimism, inflated self-esteem, poor judgment, rapid speech, racing thoughts, aggressive behavior, agitation, increased physical activity, risky behavior, spending sprees, increased drive to perform or achieve goals, increased sexual drive, decreased need for sleep, tendency to be easily distracted, and inability to concentrate. Maggie experienced many of these states while struggling with bipolar mania.

Chapter 13

DESCENT

Journal Entry - April 21, 1996

I have never been this happy in my whole life! I am now in Yosemite National Park—it is so beautiful here. I am at the Devil's Tub, sitting on the edge of a huge cliff. I am looking at a three hundred-foot cliff straight down with an amazing waterfall gushing over the edge. As I look around, I see massive mountains, deep green meadows, and a turquoise blue sky overhead. Oh, I cannot even describe how wonderful I feel. I feel as if I could fly right over these mountains if I want to. I hiked up with a bunch of young people that are from my camp, "Boys Town." There is Julian from Australia, Justin who was a pole-vaulter in high school, Heather, Bill the photographer, Ken the search-and-rescue guy, Frank who said he would take me to Hidden Falls, and my best friend and sister, Amy Anne. I wish this feeling would last forever. I feel so incredibly good. Everyone wants to know where I get my drug supplies. Drugs? This is a natural happiness! I found the real Mag here in Yosemite National Park. I am the happy Mag, a strong Mag, an adult Mag, a happy Mag—happy, confident, great, feeling independent, beautiful Margaret Ruth Hurst.

Later that evening, things took a turn for the worse. I decided that rollerblading in the dark again would be fun. As soon as I started skating around the first turn of the path, I twisted my knee and fell pretty hard on the pavement. I tweaked my knee so hard I could not even get off the ground.

The pain shot up through my leg as I tried to take my skates off. Since I could not bear any weight on my knee, I dragged my body across the path to my tent cabin. I didn't want to wake anybody for help, so I did it alone. Even though I was within seeing distance of the tent cabin, it took me an hour to scoot my way into my living quarters. The next morning, Amy didn't want to deal with me because I was irritable and was being mean to her, so I called Dad to tell him I was injured.

Journal Entry - April 22, 1996

Remember how I said I have never felt so good! Well, today was the absolute worst of all days—seriously. I woke up and had a good breakfast, then Dad took me to a Yosemite Park medical clinic. I started to feel that the doctor there was a threat to me. I threw up everywhere and screamed at him. Dr. C. said, "Maggie, if you do not calm yourself, I will have you put in lockdown!"

"What the fuck ever! What does this dipshit know anyway? A bunch of fucking bullshit, that's what. "My father luckily talked the doctor out of putting me away in the confinement area for three days.

My throat is killing me from screaming all day. I feel sick and very angry. Confused. Why can't I be alone in Yosemite? They took me away from my home, my savior, Yosemite. Plus, I had to leave all my other friends behind. I think they really will put me away. Why can't they leave me the fuck alone for a while? I need to think, I need some time, everyone get away from me dammit!

When I think about this journal entry of April 22, I can't help but think about what an awful day that must have been for Mom and Dad. They had no idea why I was acting so out of *control and why my anger spiked like never before. If it were not for Dad, I would have been locked up in the park for three days for threatening the doctor. We had to be escorted out of Yosemite by park officials. I refused to go see Mom—I don't know why—but stayed with Carrie's parents for two days. I don't recall much about those days, but I know I must have scared Carrie and her family, because at some point, they called my parents, who took me straight to the doctor.*

Amy's View – Yosemite

She was back! The sparkle in her eyes had returned. I went to Yosemite to visit her and was thrilled to see her happy. My parents felt there was something off though, so they asked me to go up for a visit to see for myself. Since I had a few days off, that seemed a great idea to me, and it was such a beautiful place to go visit! For the first two days, it was like keeping up with a car going one hundred miles per hour. She was just too happy! She wanted to run everywhere.

She kept promising people free ice cream from the stand where she worked. She began not making any sense, and I began to be scared. Only a month ago she was a zombie, and now she was out of control. She would finally get to sleep about two o'clock in the morning and then be ready to go again at 4:00 a.m.

We started to fight. I don't remember much about that last night, only that she screamed all sorts of obscenities at me and locked me out of the cabin. As I sat shivering on the steps that night, I decided that this was beyond me and called home. Dad came and rescued her—and me! As they drove away, Maggie was pounding her hands on the back window of the Blazer, screaming at the top of her lungs, "I hate you! I hate your guts! How could you do this to me?" I had ratted out my sister, but it was my only option. I might be the older sister—but sisters don't always know what to do! I surely didn't.

Maggie's Mom - Home Again From Idaho

This time, she lasted at college three days. Her call that day scared me so much I told Joe he had to go get her. My husband does not fly (after he got home from Vietnam, he announced he would never travel by air again), but on this day, he flew! With Amy's help, he flew to Spokane, rented a car, went down to Moscow, and brought her home. We settled into an uneasy coexistence. We went back to our family doctor. He gave her a new medication (this time I paid attention to the name: Zoloft) and when I said I thought she needed to talk to someone, he recommended a counselor named Kate Hack.

She went to Kate twice a week—at first, very reluctantly. She was definitely depressed. She did lots of sleeping, sometimes twelve to fifteen hours a day. Her appetite was poor; I could not find anything she wanted to eat no matter how many tricks I pulled out of my "mom bag." I took her on a little trip to visit my mother who was spending the winter in Palm Desert. We went to the movies, had neighbors visit for dinner, and tried to fill up empty days while waiting for something to get better. Maggie began to look forward to seeing Kate.

One day after a counseling session, Kate asked me to come in. She said she felt that the Zoloft was not doing the job and told me she was going to call our doctor and consult with him about trying a different medication. His office called the next day and said they would change to Effexor, a different drug for depression.

Two more weeks dragged by—and suddenly—our Maggie was back! It was as if a magic bullet had suddenly found its mark. I remember thinking, "well, thank heavens that's over!" Maggie was interested in life again—and was even quite pragmatic about having had to come home. She started reading and being interested in all sorts of things.

One day, she came home and announced that she had gone to a job interview and had landed a spring job in Yosemite Valley. She said she only intended to stay at the job until she could get back to school, but it would be great to be off on her own again. Within the week, she was gone to Yosemite. Amy came home for a few days of break and went over to see Maggie and came back with a good report: all was fine. As for us, we went to Yosemite about every weekend just to see her. She had new friends and was doing well at her job, and we all breathed a sigh of relief.

Then we got a call at two in the morning from the police chief in the valley.

He told us that if we would come and get her, he would not lock her up. Joe left immediately. It seemed that she had been rollerblading at midnight in the park, fell and twisted her knee, but when she was taken to the infirmary, she fought with the personnel. She would not talk about it when Joe got her home; she just muttered about a misunderstanding. She didn't look right; her eyes were wide open—too wide. She seemed to be staring at all of us. She went to her room and slammed the door. Then we heard her pacing around and around her room.

(One interesting thing about this incident: the week after she came home, a huge rockslide occurred in Yosemite Valley, and three people were killed, and it demolished the little ice cream shack where she had worked! If she hadn't gotten sick, she could have been killed. It was perhaps one of the first mysterious things that happened! The last thing we wanted was for our daughter to be sick, and yet if she hadn't come home, we might have lost her forever!) I took her back to our family doctor, using the excuse that he needed to check her knee. He was only with her for a few minutes before he came back out into the waiting room and sat down next to me and changed my life forever! He took my hand—and I remember thinking, Oh my god, this must be awful—and then he told me that he had misdiagnosed Maggie's condition, that she was not only depressed but was also manic, and that the medicine he had prescribed had probably brought on this full-blown attack and that he was so sorry.

He had tears in his eyes. I remember patting his knee and saying it was okay—everything would be fine, I was sure. He gave me the name of a psychiatrist in Modesto and said that Maggie needed to be evaluated and prescribed correct medication. So off we went, the two of us in the car together heading home. Maggie looked at me with her big blue eyes and said, "Mom, Dr. M. called me a maniac!" I looked over at her and said, "No, honey, the word is manic, and that is totally different than maniac." "Oh," she said, "that's okay then," and promptly fell asleep. I, on the other hand, cried silently all the way home, knowing that I didn't have a clue about whether or not manic and maniac were the same or not.

The next six weeks were terrible. The psychiatrist in Modesto saw Maggie right away. I am sure our doctor twisted his arm to get us in so soon. The psychiatrist saw her by herself for about twenty minutes and then called me into the room. He confirmed that Maggie was manic depressive (the new term is bipolar). That means the patient has ups and downs—not just downs. He told us that lithium had been used for over fifty years as the correct medication. He said the biggest problem was finding the right dosage, so that meant that they would start her on a low dose and then increase it slowly until her symptoms decreased.

Maggie was walking around the office while he talked to me, and then she opened the door and walked out. I started to ask a question—I don't even remember what it was about—and he looked at me, laid his pen on his desk, and stated that he could not answer because he could not violate patient-client privilege! I was stunned; she was my daughter. He said she was nineteen and there was nothing he could do. I somehow managed to totter out of his office and paid the $200 bill for the visit. I found Maggie, who was already walking down the street, talked her into the car, and drove the sixty miles home. She slept. I cried.

Really—the next six weeks, that was all I did. I cried. Maggie was up twenty to twenty-two hours a day. She said she didn't want to stay with us. She talked a neighbor into letting her stay with them. She lasted three days. She went on to two more friends' houses. Both ended in disaster, so she had to come home. Joe and I hung on to her. He somehow managed to keep our business going during the day, and I just stayed with her. She called friends, got rides to town, and would just walk the streets all day. She wanted to go out every night and tell us she had been invited to parties. We finally realized we couldn't keep it up, and we needed help; we needed someone to keep her safe when we couldn't. Over a course of weeks, we hired two or three of her friends from school to just stay with her. We paid the princely sum of ten dollars an hour and told them to just stay with her, go to the beach with her, go to the lake with her, drive her around in our car, and take her to clubs; they just had to keep her safe. Each one said a variation of "You mean you just want us to go have fun and you will pay us for that?" They all took off happily; but in quick succession, each one gave up after a few days. I learned to have the next "pigeon" on deck ready to go. All the time, we were also driving periodically to the psychiatrist. He continued to counsel Maggie and increase her dosage. I was left in the waiting room, I was kept in the dark about what was happening, and I was paying the bill.

Chapter 14

CONCERN

I am getting better! Today I went to Dr. Minner. I am so much calmer! I know I can talk the doctor into getting me back to Yosemite.

I am okay. Dr. Minner says if I go back to Yosemite, I will probably get into more serious trouble. He thinks I need to check in to a hospital just for one night so the staff can evaluate me. Whatever that problem is, I have no idea. I don't feel depressed at all. I feel very happy. In the meantime, my dad says I can stay with Carrie's parents.

I don't want to stay with Mom. She is all worried and frazzled. I just want to go back to Yosemite with my friends and the tent cabin. I feel very calm.

Well, I didn't exactly get to go back to Yosemite. By this time, I was way out of control. I couldn't stand still for even a moment. Everything I did was at warp speed, from talking to people to making plans for my future to cleaning myself. I couldn't hold a thought for any length of time. Even when I tried to slow myself down, it was impossible. I was headed for a complete disaster—I didn't know I was getting sicker by the minute. I would lie down at night, but I could not sleep. Ideas would run through my mind at what seemed like a million miles per hour. I wanted to go to Hollywood to be a movie star, then the next instant, I had a plan to be a singer, and then I would imagine that I would be a star runner again. These plans seemed so attainable and realistic, but then again, everything I did seemed normal to me—but not to anybody else. My condition would only get worse.

Journal Entry - April 25

I am making big progress! It is so beautiful right now!

Journal Entry - April 28, 1996

I have spent three days at the Webbers. Terry and Marilynn have been very kind to me. I told Carrie's parents everything she has been doing at college. Everything - I really ratted her out! I know I betrayed her, but I also know it was for the best. Last night, I hung out with some guys I used to go to high school with. I think they were very surprised to see me. My ex-boyfriend Nathan was there. It was great to see him again. After staying with Carrie's parents, I spent one night at the Rodgers. Actually, I didn't make it through the night.

I was told not to use the phone, and I did. I called my old sorority and cussed them out. Anyway, Jeanette found me on the phone, and I just lost it at her. Dad had to come pick me up. I was yelling, they were yelling, what a fucking mess. So I am fucking angry right now, I cannot even think straight. Everyone is telling me to calm down. Well, I am calming down; I just want some goddamn, fucking freedom back! I could not even leave my room all night because Dad slept outside my door. I even tried to escape my room by using the fire escape ladder outside my two-story window. I guess Dad heard me. Mom got up and started crying, acting all worried. What is the big problem anyway? I just wanted to take a walk by myself in the fresh air. I feel completely trapped. Nathan is coming over today, so I will be fine.

NOTE: Those who have been intimately acquainted with persons suffering bipolar disorder can observe that one of the most problematic aspects of mania is that the manic state is a compulsive high in which the patient is totally immersed. The patient lacks a sense of responsibility to others. It is like being caught up in a tidal wave— exhilarating, compelling, and very dangerous.

Maggie's Mom - The First Hospitalization

Maggie was not getting better—if anything, she was getting worse. She was not sleeping. Her face was breaking out; She was gaining weight. Then, the worst of all (to her way of thinking), her beautiful long hair was falling out in handfuls! The psychiatrist just told me these were all side effects of lithium, and we just had to soldier on; and he kept increasing her dosage.

One morning, I heard a funny sound from the bathroom and went up to discover Maggie sitting naked in the middle of the floor, quietly sobbing. She looked up at me and said, "Mom, this medicine is supposed to make me live again—but I think I am dying anyway!" I got down and held her awhile, frantically trying to figure out what to say and finally offered to call Dr. M. again and see if he had suggestions other than visiting the psychiatrist again. She jumped at the idea. He got right on the phone and listened to me—and then said he thought that Maggie had had enough of trying to do this by herself—and that he thought we should take her to the hospital so that they could help her get stabilized.

I went back upstairs and told Maggie what he said, and wonder of wonders, she agreed to go. Our local hospital had a psychiatric ward on the third floor; but other than that it was right here in town—I knew nothing about it. I called Joe, and he came home and helped me dress her. Then we took her to the hospital and admitted her. She was quiet and seemed hopeful.

Maggie was in the hospital for ten days. Many things happened; I will simply list them in no particular order because it was all kind of a fog for me.

I spent lots of time sitting in the hall waiting for her to see me. She hated the staff, and the staff seemed to hate her after a while. I kept telling myself that they knew best, that they were treating her so harshly because she deserved it.

But it was still hard to watch them yell at her.

She loved all the other patients. She tried to organize their lives for them.

In fact, for the next three months, strangers would show up at our store, saying they had been promised a job with us as soon as they got out of the third floor of the hospital! Maggie also staged an insurrection among the patients. Finally, Maggie was kept alone on one side of the floor, and everyone else was crammed up in the other.

While Maggie had few visitors, she did have two who were wonderful. Mrs.Cavanero, her former Math teacher from Sonora High, seemed to know what to do; she came every other day with children's books and read them to Maggie.

Children's books! Who would have thought that would give peace and calmness for even just twenty or thirty minutes at a time! I owe her a debt of gratitude that can never be fully repaid! Mr. Roeber, her coach from high school, was her other visitor. He was a faithful friend to Maggie, and I think he was beginning to wonder if there were other kids in his program like Maggie—especially after we had talked about Maggie's drive to win and how it had seemed to be her drug of choice for trying to battle whatever was happening to her.

She made a friend—Julie—who was ten years older but looked the same age, and she is still a friend to this day! I fell in love with Julie too, but for another reason; if she could make it to age thirty being bipolar, then maybe Maggie could live and find a life too! As you can tell, I was grasping at straws.

One day, the hospital called and asked to come in to see the administrator.

I remember thinking that they probably wanted to know how we intended to pay for Maggie's care. When I got there, there was a crowd of people around a table, and I thought, my god, it's an intervention! Then I was informed that they wanted me to be on the hospital board of directors—and had no idea my daughter was locked up on the floor above us! I remember laughing slightly hysterically, and then gently saying no.

I remember driving by one day to see that there were signs in the windows up on her floor and that they all said HELP! in her handwriting. By the time I parked and went up, the staff had taken the signs down. They were angry and said I could not see her—that she was being punished.

I did finally get to talk to a psychiatrist at the hospital; she was in charge of the third floor and called me in for a meeting. She told me that Maggie was definitely bipolar and that she had a conference with the doctor in Modesto and felt that we were on the right track. Then she asked me an odd question, "Who in your family—or in your husband's family—is or was mentally ill?" I was stunned—and answered, "No one." She looked skeptical and then went on to other subjects, but that question nagged me.

Later that evening, when I was talking to my mother, I brought it up and said, "Wasn't that the oddest thing for her to ask me?" There was silence on the phone, and then my mother dropped a bomb: *"Well, there was your uncle Jim!"* I couldn't believe it. *"Mom! How could you not have told me?"* I yelled over the phone. She said that they just didn't talk about family matters like that and that it never dawned on her that Maggie's medical condition was somehow related to her brother's mental problem. I told her I needed to think and I would call her back. Finally, when I calmed down long enough to listen, I called back and found out about Uncle Jim.

Jim was the third child in my mother's family. There were five boys and my mother. When he was a college freshman, and living in Seattle, he tried to hold up a city bus by holding his hand in his pocket like a gun. The bus driver took one look and just drove the bus to a police station. There, the police chief called my grandfather and had him come and take Jim home. The treatment of choice in the late 1930s was a state mental hospital and electroshock therapy. (Since then, in my reading, I found out that as awful as that sounds, mainly due to the book One Flew Over the Cuckoo's Nest, some people who got the electroshock treatment actually got better, and it turns out the ones who did were the ones who were manic-depressives!) It actually helped Uncle Jim.

He was hospitalized for six months and then went back to college. He graduated in chemistry, married, had two boys, and worked as a chemist for a large food company for his entire career. Mom told me he would be fine; but then, every five or six years, he would go back into a hospital for more treatment. He died in his sixties of a heart attack. Neither of his children had children— something I have thought about many times; was their childhood so hard that they consciously made the decision not to pass on the gene that they too carried? Or was their childlessness just a quirk of fate? I have never asked either of my two cousins. It seems too personal a question, even from me - and even now.

Now I had another burden to bear: not only was my daughter mentally ill, but I had carried the very gene that caused it. I think I cried for three days. I know I yelled at my mother that she should have told me; and finally, I went to Kate, Maggie's counselor, on my own. She helped me to see that, yes, I had passed on a bad gene, but I had also given Maggie my blonde hair and blue eyes. After a while, I just "let go" of that awful realization and just went back to keeping on.

The business office called and asked me to come in to make arrangements.

I gave them all the paperwork from our insurance company, and when the woman at the window saw which insurance we had, she said, "Oh, Lisa handles them," and called Lisa over. She looked familiar to me, and then I remembered that Lisa had been a babysitter for us when the kids were little, and Joe and I were able to go out for a date night. She told me she was so sorry about Maggie being on the third floor but that she did know how to handle our company and would get right on it.

After some resistance, they did pay their 80 percent, and we were able to pay the rest. At the time, the bill still seemed outrageous; little did we know what was ahead of us! One evening about eight, the phone rang, and it was the head nurse on the third floor. She said Maggie was ready to come home! I remember saying incredulously, "You mean she is cured?" There was silence, and then the nurse said quietly, "Well, no, not exactly. Just have your husband come and pick her up." It turned out that the health care system had come into the picture, and the situation became very complicated.

A patient advocate had come to the third floor. Her job was to make sure all the patients knew their rights. She told Maggie she didn't have to stay if she didn't want to—and that all she had to do was sign a few papers, and she could walk out. We called Dr. M. and the psychiatrist in Modesto and the head of the psychiatric unit, but there was nothing we could do: Maggie was over eighteen, the age of consent for that kind of thing. I remember yelling, "How can you let her just walk out into the darkness and take no responsibility for her?" But the advocate just turned and walked out of the room.

Joe and I begged Maggie to come home with us. We followed her along the street for about three blocks before she took pity on us and got into the car. We drove home in silence, understanding that we had entered a new and very uneasy period with Maggie; she now had power over us, and she had learned how to use it!

Chapter 15

FIFTY-ONE-FIFTY

Journal Entry - Monday, April 29, 1996

Around 2:00 pm I am right now sitting on the third floor of a mental institution— the psychiatric ward at Tuolumne General Hospital in Sonora. I guess they think I am 51/50 another term for going crazy! It is very interesting I must say. First of all, there are tons of rules to follow.

If I go to the bathroom, I have to be escorted; if I want to watch television, I have to wait for TV time; and so on. The rules and hours are endless. I just sit and stare at the clock, wondering if I will ever get out of this fucking hell that I am in. I get so pissed off even if I try to stay calm. There are only certain times for meals and snacks.

A nurse has to be present if you want to shave your legs. If I have to go number 2, I have to leave the door open. There are two sides to the mental ward, and I wish I was on the other. There is freedom on the other side. The patients on the other side have that freedom because they are not a threat to themselves or others. They obviously think I am a fucking threat! What the fuck ever. If they want to see a fucking threat, I'll show them a fucking threat. My papers actually say that I am a danger to others and myself! I just find that hard to believe.

Little old me wanting to hurt myself hardly seems right. I know there is nothing wrong with me. I will get out of here by tomorrow, I just know it. All I want to do in my life is be successful. Is that so hard for people to understand? I just need a chance to show everyone that I am all right. I need my mom to know that I love her, and I just want everything to be all right.

The patients here are really creeping me out. There is this one guy named Steve that has me really disturbed. He is sitting across from me as I write this journal. He is talking to his dead brother in the wall. He says, "Hey, bro, you have to get me out of this joint. How have you been, man? I have been doing great, but I need to get back to my work." Then Steve says to me, "Hey, Maggie, what the hell are you writing in that book of yours? You're freaking me out! Tell me now this instant!" I tried to ignore him, but he just kept at it. Then he tried to grab it away from me as I screamed. The white coats came rushing in from their glassed-in office and tackled Steve to the ground. He put up quite a fuss yelling and screaming all the way down the hall. The white coats dragged him into the solitary confinement room and strapped him down. It was quite a shocking sight for me to see. There was no way in hell I ever wanted to end up in that place. As quickly as the white coats came out, they went back to their glass palace. They just sit there and stare at us like we are rats in a laboratory.

Well, after all the excitement of the afternoon, I have to go pee. First, though, I have to tap on the glass and wait for the fat-ass nurse to wobble her way out to escort me to the bathroom! please, god, let me go home and have my freedom! It is now 3:30 a.m., and this place is really scary. I have met just about every patient on my side of the ward. I have already told you about Steve. He also told me he was a millionaire. I highly doubt that. If he were, he wouldn't be in this shitty place. He has deep scars all over his face, his hair is thin and matted all over, and his entire body is very frail and worn-out looking. I think he lives on the street. Another patient, Chris, is an awkward short fat guy with brown hair and brown eyes. He just mimics everything I do, which I find totally annoying. I just wish he would leave me alone for just one fucking minute. I think he is about thirty years old or so. Then there is Kristy, my roommate.

She is recovering from trying to kill herself with an overdose of aspirin. She is about 5'2", with dark brown eyes and beautiful long brown hair. She has two kids and a husband at home and is thirty-two years old. She doesn't talk much.

She pretty much keeps to herself in our room, so I don't bother her. I only know a little bit about her because Chris told me. Then there is James. He is tall, dark, and handsome with round glasses. I guess he also tried to kill himself with drugs and alcohol. That seems to be the trend in this hellhole. Anne is yet another patient that is fat, short, and extremely ugly. She just sits by the phone and pretends to be talking to people. Nobody pays her any attention. She won't let anyone else use the phone. I think she has obsessive-compulsive disorder.

She is always pulling strands of hair out of her head (and lining them up on the floor), arranging the furniture in the television room, and washing her hands constantly. If I go near the phone, she screams at me. She is definitely one to stay away from. She is in her thirties I think. That's everyone as far as I know on our side of the ward. We have had no contact yet with the other side of the ward. I can see them across the glass partition, but we never get to talk to them.

Bill is our ward nurse right now. They go in shifts. So far, Bill is my favorite one. He talks like a real person. He jokes with us and talks about our goals and what we are going to do once we leave. Right now, I am locked in my little square white room. It is so quiet I could hear a pin drop. Kristy is dead asleep and doesn't make a sound. I am so bored; I wish I could at least watch some television. I think I hear somebody coming down the hall. I guess I will have to write more later, since there is nothing to do. "Lights out," the nurse calls.

Everything goes black after that. I barely hear Kristy breathing as I lie wide awake wondering what will become of me.

NOTE: Another aspect of mania is self-justification combined with very limited self-awareness. These combine with delusional thinking. The "enthusiasm" that mania generates is often felt as extreme well-being by the patient. Since such a person feels that they are full of positive energy and has no qualms about her actions, anyone countering those actions—or who limits the patient's sphere of action—is seen as an enemy or, at the very least, a wrongdoer. Thus, mania carries its own false ethos, and those transgressing that ethos often receive a bitterly angry response from the patient. (Information gleaned from direct observation and from bipolar.com.)

Chapter 16

RULES

This place really sucks! I guess that is all the more reason to follow their stupid procedures and get the fuck out! The fucking nurses don't let you sleep in. Then right away, I have to be escorted to the shower and practically be watched the entire time. I have no privacy at all. I feel embarrassed and scared. Why are the nurses allowed to watch us shower? All there is in the shower is a bar of soap.

Today, after cleaning myself up, we were all escorted to the cafeteria. The food was totally gross. The fruit was sour, the toast cold, and the eggs runny. I just shoved the food around on my plate until we were shuffled down to our first awful group meeting of the day.

"Maggie, let's start with you," the nurse urged. I shouted back, "All right, you want me to start, I will begin. My name is Maggie, I am nineteen years old, and I don't know why I am here. They tell me there is something wrong with me, but I feel fine. If I could just get out of this fucking loony bin, I would be fine!" The nurse wasn't too keen on my answer and asked Chris to volunteer with a more positive attitude. The meeting went on like this for about an hour, and then we were dismissed for free time. I immediately ran to the phone before Anne could get there. I started calling everyone I could think of.

First, I called my friend Jesarah. She was getting married on Friday.

"I just know I will be there. I just need to check out of here, and I will be as good as new," I lied.

Later on, a bunch of friends came to visit. Nathan, JuJu, Sara, Jesarah, Coach Roeber, Mom, Dad, and Tom all came for a visit.

It was great to see everybody. The only disappointment was that the doctor said I was not ready to go home and that they had to do more observation and come up with a diagnosis for me. I was a little depressed after that. It felt like I had been there weeks already.

I also had to take a drug test today. I thought that was way out of line. Of course, I have no say about what goes on here. I have never touched any kind of drug. That makes me so angry that nobody will believe me. The nurse told me it was just procedure. Procedure—I have begun to despise that word. Everything around this joint is procedure! Steve told me I act like I was on crank. What the fuck does Steve know about me? I am acting just fine. I sure hope I get to leave soon.

I feel so sick May 1, 1996. It is May Day, and I am stuck in this miserable hole of a place.

As a little girl, I would make bouquets with Amy and Mom and pass them out to all the neighbors. It seems like such a distant memory now. I wish I could turn back time. Today was yet another endless journey. The hours went by so slowly I thought that maybe the clock stopped. The hospital is such a lonely place. Just white walls, bars on the widows, and beds bolted to the floor. It is 3:43 a.m., and I have a temperature of 100.1; the nurse just took it. I have been getting hot and cold *flashes all night long. When the next shift of nurses came, they were horrible to me. They said to go back to bed and stay there.*

It is so lonely in there now that Kristy has left. Even though we didn't talk much, it was nice to have her in there. Now, I sit on my bed and write since there is nothing else to do. I should try to sleep though.

Good night for now.

Chapter 17

BLACKOUT

Journal Entry - May 2, 1996

This day felt like the longest day of my life. I really hate it here with a passion I cannot begin to describe. This morning started out especially bad. The nurse gave me some kind of drug that didn't agree with my stomach. I immediately began throwing up. Then I began to walk down the hall toward the bathroom, and I blacked out.

When I came to, I was clammy and dizzy. The nurses tried the best they could to carry me back to bed. What are they giving me to make me this sick so fast? I feel like I am a character in "One Flew Over the Cuckoo's Nest." I called an old running buddy, Joanna. She and I cried on the phone for what seemed like forever. She kept telling me to hang in there and everything would be fine. I didn't believe her though. I can't remember when things were fine in my life. It has been so long since I have felt like myself. The doctor told me they need to do more tests. I am getting tired of all the observing and tests.

Why can't they just figure out what they needed from me and let me go? They say I am not well mentally. Well, I guessed that is the case since that's what every nurse tells me in this godforsaken place.

I saw Dad and Mom today. They tried to be positive for me. "Mags, I know you're going to be fine. Just do what the doctors tell you, and take your medicine," Mom pleaded. I sighed.

"Mom, if it were that easy, I would, but it is a living hell in here. I can't stand the doctors, nurses, or the food." Mom and Dad stayed for a little while and then were told it was time to leave.

I cannot even go to the bathroom without asking. My math teacher from high school, Mrs. Cavanero, stopped by to see me, which was a nice change.

She read me some funny Dr. Seuss books and even sneaked me a candy bar. My old boyfriend, Nathan, stopped by to say hello too. Later on, Chuck Brewster, one of my biggest running fans, came by for a few minutes. "Get out of here, kid, you don't belong in this nasty place," he said under his breath. He told me that as soon as I get out, he will take me water-skiing. That sounds so good right now: to be out on the lake with the wind in my face. In this stark hole of a place, there is no fresh air and no wind—just the stale smell of the patients sticking to the chairs. The living room area is really bare: no pictures to look at, a single couch in the middle of the room facing the television, and two worn-out, dull, gray chairs. We almost never get to watch TV. Even when we do get to watch it, Ann takes it over, so we can't watch what we want to anyway. I watch the clock a lot, thinking that maybe that will make time speed up and I will get out sooner. That only makes things worse; the second hand takes hours to get around the clock face.

It is hard to believe I have been here four long days. It seems like months since I was working in Yosemite. I wonder what my little camp of people is doing. Are they banging on their drums in the clearing, hiking up to the waterfalls, or maybe swimming in the river? At least they're not with a bunch of controlling nurses and crazy people talking to walls. I definitely think this is the toughest race I have ever been in. So far, I am losing badly too. I feel as though everything I do is wrong. I really don't understand why I am here.

Not having any outside time is just too much to bear. When I ask the nurses if I can go outside, they don't hear me; I think they just ignore me. I wonder what makes a nurse want to work in a psychiatric ward anyway. There are so many more jobs out there that are in a better atmosphere. Maybe they need to have control over other people. I bet they lack control in their own lives, so they want to control others. That makes a lot more sense to me.

When I talk to the staff, or even to my family, they all look at me like I have the devil in me or something. I just can't figure it out. I used to see my family as loving, kind, and helpful; but now I see them as the ones that put me in this place to torture me. They try to control my wonderful ideas. I feel like the entire world is against me. I feel if I could be just given the chance, I could show everyone how great I am and see my awesome powers. I hope these feelings that I have stay a long time so I can prove to everyone that I can do anything.

The problem is, a lot of times, I cannot think clearly. The staff keeps giving me drugs that make things seem hazy. I feel as if my mind, body, and spirit are slowly slipping away.

Chapter 18

"NURSE RATCHED"

I was just told by a nurse named Pat that I come across as a mean person! I feel bad that I hurt her feelings, but at the same time, she was mean to me. I have never been told that I am mean by anybody. This truly shocks me. In the past, people have always commented on how kind I am. I think she is mistaken and needs to get to know me before she makes random statements like that. My goal has always been to help people, not hurt them.

Jim, the alcoholic who tried to kill himself, left the hospital this afternoon. He was very kind to all of us and to the staff. Yesterday, we spent time together watching the movie What About Bob? It was funny to watch a movie about a crazy man when here we sat in a crazy house! Right now on the tube, the movie The Silence of the Lambs is playing. What kind of a hospital is this anyhow? Learn how to be a psycho 101! I just looked out the barred window. Jim is still sitting there on the curb. I wonder who is going to pick him up. I wonder if he is going to stay off alcohol. I sure hope he does, because he has a family back home.

Today has been the best day on the ward so far. I started a Scrabble tournament for all the patients. A new patient has joined our group today, which also makes life here more interesting. Her name is Patty, and boy, does she have a shit load of problems. She talks to herself, has no self-confidence, and looks like she has not taken a shower in weeks. She smells terrible.

I am still the youngest here. I think the staff is making a huge mistake by keeping me in here with a bunch of crazy old people. I got tired of Scrabble, so I talked Patty into cleaning herself up, and then I practiced makeup on her. I think she has never worn makeup before. I made her look pretty good compared to how she looked like a few hours before. She got all excited when she saw what I did to her.

Shelly Ann is the meanest of everyone here. Since she guards the phone for herself all the time, but she never really talks with anybody, she just pretends. I call her the Receptionist. Because she guards the phone every damn minute. "Get off the fucking phone, Shelly Ann. You need to share it, and I know you're not talking to anybody!" "I don't have to listen to a word you say, you crazy, good-for nothing maniac!" she yelled back. Then I just grabbed the phone away from Shelly Ann. She started screaming at the top of her lungs.

Well, that got the attention of the white coats at once. Pat came waddling out from behind her thick glass barrier. "Both of you, stop yelling at each other at once. Maggie, you stay away from Shelly Ann. Stop bugging her!" Pat commanded in a sharp tone. "Me, why the fuck are you telling me to stop? It is Shelly Ann who hogs the damn phone. Tell her to go fuck off!" I shouted back. Pat shut me down. She said, "That is it, Maggie. You are going to your room for a time-out." I can't fucking believe that now I have to sit in my square-box room with stale air because of that lunatic Shelly Ann. I can't believe this is happening; we are treated like first graders. Because of the uproar, my phone rights have been taken away, and I am allowed no magazines, no TV, and no going to play with other patients. At least I have this journal to write in.

Well, at least we did have some patients get to leave in the past couple of days. Besides Jim, the alcoholic, and Kristy, my roommate, Sal went back to Sacramento, and Jody left. The staff does not tell us when we will get to go home or who gets to go when. When someone goes, they are just gone when we wake up. A little while ago, my friend Dani stopped by my window and drew up some signs for me.

I thought she was so sneaky writing her messages on the whiteboard.

I wish I could be with her. We have so many great plans for doing things in the city when I get out. She left, and then I was alone again until the nurse came by for lights-out.

Journal Entry - May 5, 1996

There are not many of us left in here. Just Steve, Patty, Shelly Ann, Kris, and me. I can hardly wait to get some fresh air. The nurse said I have to earn a pass to go outside. I guess there are levels you have to earn to get out. I don't think I am even close to whatever level I need to get out into fresh air. Right now, I am sitting in the TV room at 11:44 p.m., and I am finally wearing down a bit. Maybe it is all that medication they are giving me. Today I didn't take my morning dose.

I pretended to swallow and then spit the pill back out when the nurse wasn't looking.

There is a regular drug trade in here. Some patients, like Steve, save up a bunch and then trade with others like Shelly Anne. I don't know why they want each other's meds. I know I have said this so many times before, but I want to get out of here so bad it hurts. I never want my freedom taken away again. I want to follow the rules so I can get out and stay out. I have missed so much since I have been in here. I lost my job in Yosemite, and I wasn't able to go to my friend Jesarah's wedding.

I have known Jesarah since I was five years old. We grew up in private school together and ended up going to high school together too. We were not close later on, but we have always kept in touch.

Tomorrow, Amy is bringing in Burger King. She has to bring enough food for everybody because that is the rule here. It is so nice of her to do that for me. I know that at Yosemite, I was mean to her, and I just feel terrible about it. I am glad she is coming for a visit. Well, the nurse has called for lights-out for the hundredth time, so enough writing for tonight.

Thinking back on those long days and nights on the third floor of Tuolumne General gives me the chills. With time going slower than a snail, having hardly anything to do but think about where I was, and fighting with the other patients, it is a wonder that I was able to survive those two long weeks. How I coped through all the confusion and emotional pain, I will never know. The journal is the one thing that kept me busy and at least somewhat focused. I wrote down conversations, observations of what was going on, and random thoughts. By writing everything down on paper, I passed the time, and once I wrote it all down, I could at least see it all a little more clearly, and my situation seemed a little more tolerable. Writing in the journal was a way of purging all my anger.

I know that my hospitalization was hardest for my parents. They felt guilty putting me in the hospital, but it was their only choice; otherwise, I probably would have run off somewhere and hurt myself. We all needed to find out what was destroying me. This illness was wrecking my whole life. I was losing friends, I lost my college scholarship, my personality had become strange, and my family was hanging on by a mere thread.

I was surprised that Carrie remained my friend, especially as had I called her from the hospital and yelled at her for no reason at all. I knew I had a good friend when she stuck by me through all of that. It is hard to think back and remember that things were only going to get worse for my family and me. No one knew that, in the months to come, we were going to go further into the cavern of doom. I wasn't even close to being out of the woods yet.

Carrie Webber – What About Me?

"So what about me? Did anyone give a second thought of me and how I was feeling and what I was going through? I mean, I am a part of this. I was considered part of the family, if only the best friend." These were the very real and selfish thoughts running through my mind every minute of every day. I was in utter turmoil, sick to my stomach, and feeling as if I was going down right alongside my best friend. I was confused and angry, bitter and hurt, and probably the most helpless I have ever felt. I won the award for pity that year.

And I also won the grand prize for "most useless feeling." I was a winner, indeed, of all the things that make you completely miserable. I was a miserable human being knowing that my life was never going to be the same again.

It all started eleven years ago. Second grade is the grade to define all grades in elementary school. Okay, maybe I am just being dramatic, but for me, second grade was the year I was introduced to my best friend, Maggie. I didn't know that the lunch we shared or the drinking fountain we fought over or even the four square game we battled tirelessly to win would be the beginning of an amazing friendship.

Carrie and me when we were 19 in Mexico. (Courtesy the Hurst family)

Maggie was a tall, gangly blonde with knobby knees and a feisty personality that you couldn't miss in a crowded room. I, on the other hand, was on the shorter side of the height chart, with blonde hair and the muscular build of a young gymnast. In other words, I had big thighs and a butt to match. My mom called us Mutt and Jeff, appropriately named. Maggie and I formed a friendship over the next ten years that was based on one word: fun.

We even developed our own motto, "Living on the edge." We hardly did anything dangerous, but we liked the implication. We did everything our imaginations would allow us, from exploring gold mines and making forts to inspecting every inch of our mountainous backyards, all in the name of fun. We would do the goofiest things just so we could laugh. We were the picture of a great friendship. We never tired of each other's company; we never fought and rarely disagreed about anything. I was the happiest when I was with Maggie.

So why did it have to change? To recount all the events that lead up to Maggie's departure from reality still makes my heart hurt. Even though some of the details are hazy in my mind now, they are so fresh in my heart that it still hurts to think about them. She had left her body, and someone else had taken over, causing destruction and pain. She was unrecognizable to those who knew her, leaving them wondering what in the world was going on. She was my best friend and yet became a total stranger. I found it very difficult to be around during the initial episode. It was hard to separate the person I knew from the person whom she had become. I wanted to talk to her like I always did, but she couldn't communicate the same way. Our conversations were tainted and awkward, full of anger and rage. For the first time in our lives, we fought seriously. She would call me on the phone and begin to curse at me and tell me what a horrible person I was. It was a constant battle on the phone, and our talks were filled with accusations and hate, mostly on her part.

Eventually, my reactions to these conversations changed as I began to understand what was going on with Maggie—but my first reaction was disbelief.

I didn't know what to say, and I couldn't believe these words were coming from her mouth. I stuttered, groaned, and sat dumbfounded like a whipped puppy at my end of the phone line. After a few weeks of this, my response to her became an eye for an eye. I didn't know what was going on in her brain, or her life for the matter, so I lashed out in anger. *If she said a hurtful word, then I responded with one of my own. It was a futile and pointless yelling match that ended in someone hanging up—usually me—and being frustrated and hurt in the end.*

Later, I came to the realization that she had no control over her emotions or even her mind, which meant that the words that came from her mouth were not hers. The best way I found to communicate and deal with the phone calls was to sit in silence and wait until she was done or became frustrated from the silence.

It was then that I would tell her how much I loved her, how much I cared, and how much I wanted her to get help.

I felt that the only way I could love her and help her was through tough love.

I would tell her that I had to hang up, that I couldn't talk to her when she was like this, and that it wasn't fair to me and it wasn't doing her any good either.

Through her yelling and pleading for me not to do it, I would tell her good-bye, and I would hang up the phone. It got to the point where I would screen her calls and tell my roommates to tell her that I wasn't home.

I don't know if I did this more for her benefit or mine. I always said I did it for her, that she needed help, and I wasn't able to give it to her the way she needed. Deep down, I think I did it for me too. I couldn't handle the words that she said or the tone of her voice. I just couldn't do it all the time; I needed a break every once in a while, and looking back, I truly believe that it was the right thing to do for both of us. I was a crutch for her, an excuse, and a place to vent her crazy thoughts and ideas, but I wasn't strong enough to handle it all the time, so distance and limited communication seemed to work best.

Don't get me wrong, I wasn't ignoring the problem or her, but self preservation must take precedence during these life crises in order to make it through to the other side with that person. You can't go down with the ship.

If you did, who would be there to throw the life preserver? You stand on the shore with the life ring in your hand ready to throw when she is ready to catch.

You stand on firm ground and allow the waves to drown out the words of hurt, but never lose sight of the one you love who is in danger of drowning. You let the swirling tide of her family and doctors bring her closer to the shore, while you stand there cheering her on and encouraging her to finish the race and to literally fight for her life. Then at just the right time, you throw that life ring with all your might, and pull. You pull and pull and never give up until she reaches the shore and stands firm right beside you. Patience must be your motto, and strength must be your prayer. You must love unconditionally and forgive without hesitation, and then you do it over and over again. You can't be bitter or hold things against this person; you must let go of every hurt and focus on the person you love and their recovery. You have to fight! So what about me? What about my feelings and hurts and wants? What about the day I said good-bye to Maggie, thinking it would be the last time I saw her alive? And what about the day I sat on their porch with her mom, and we both cried knowing that we had lost her, and we thought it was forever? What about the hospital visits and that long horrible road to regaining her mind? And what about what this meant to our relationship, was it going to be different, was she ever going to be the same? What about all the questions? Well, I will tell you what. Maggie, my best friend, is a fighter. She got the help she needed and fought with every ounce of her being to get better. It wasn't pretty, but it was all her. She came out the other side of this, maybe a little changed, but she came through it with her family and friends right beside her.

Not only that, but I came through this process changed as well. I understand forgiveness in a completely new light. I know the meaning of grace in a deeper and more profound way than ever before. I love my friend in a way that can only be described by emotions; no words I could write would describe this feeling. I will defend our friendship and her character to the grave. She is my best friend, my sister. That's what about me.

Celebrating my 30th birthday with Carrie. (Courtesy Carrie Webber)

Chapter 19

AIR!

Journal Entry - May 6, 1996

I want fresh air! My room looks so beautiful right now. Mom brought me a Saks Fifth Avenue catalog, and I taped the photos all over my room. That gives the room some color and style. I am tired of looking at white walls and barred windows. I love Saks; it is one of my favorite stores.

Mom also brought me pictures of Jesarah's wedding. She looked like she was really happy in those pictures.

Mom and Dad bought me some pretty pink lilies too. It is the first pleasant smell I have encountered in days, and is another thing I have taken for granted: nice smells of home, fresh air, flowers, and perfumes. I didn't know how lucky I was just to be able to inhale all those wonderful scents. Now that I am in this hospital, I smell cleaning products, and that is about it. I do have a nice view out my window though. There is a lovely maroon flowery tree that fills up most of the window. Beyond the tree, I can see cars parked at the hospital, a small lawn area with flowers along the border, and people driving by on their way to work. I wish I could be in one of those cars. I could at least be on my way to some place and have a purpose to go somewhere.

Steve went totally nuts this afternoon. It was very sad to see. He wanted to see his dead brother again and just started screaming at the top of his lungs. All the white coats rushed us into our rooms and locked us in, which made me quite nervous. They dragged Steve down the hall, and he was fighting them with all he had. I think they put him in the padded room with restraints on. Even though he was at the other end of the hall, we could still hear him cursing and yelling.

I wish I hadn't had to witness such a scene. It was shocking as any movie, but way too real for me.

After a while, we were finally let out of our rooms. Patty wanted me to do her hair, which gave me something to do. She must have really liked it because she kept telling all the nurses to check out her new style. The nurses have taken away my TV time again because they said I was being difficult. They have so many rules here that I can't remember them all. Every time anybody breaks a rule, they get something taken away from them. I feel like I get picked on the most. I don't see anybody else in trouble. So now, I just write in my journal trying to pass the time. I wish I could speed it up. It just seems like time is at a standstill in here. I'm sure that the nurses think they win when they take a privilege away from me. They all get that kind of smirk on their faces that says, "I showed you, little missy." I don't let them see that I am disappointed. I can't let them think they are ahead.

I hope some more of my friends would stop by the window. I get a real kick out of their whiteboard messages. I feel awfully lonely right now. The nurses have also taken away my visitor and phone times. Maybe the patients that got out will stop by for a visit. I guess they wouldn't, though, after being in this miserable place. It is hard not being able to go outside. I have forgotten what fresh air is like. Even a crack from a window would be nice, but everything is shut up tight around here. I miss my cats, Matilda and Fanny. Maybe when I leave here,

Dani and I will rent an apartment together in San Francisco. I just have to figure out how I can get out of this place; there must be a loophole of some kind. I feel like a caged animal in a zoo. Why does life have to be so complicated, with controlling people telling you what to do, how to live your life, how to act, and where to go? Oh, let me be, world. Just leave me alone.

Please.

Chapter 20

SNACK TIME

Journal Entry - May 7, 1996

It is now snack time! Wow! Could my life be any more exciting that I am writing about snack time of all things? I can't help but wonder what my friends are up to. Last year at this time, I had a boyfriend, I was getting ready for section finals for track and state meet, and I was looking forward to graduating high school. Now I am being called manic and am locked up on the third floor of a mental institution with my life in complete shambles. How could my life change so much in such a short time? I feel that almost everything is out of my control. I can't even go outside for heaven's sake. At a time like this, it is so hard to look forward to the future.

Will I have a future worth looking forward to? I do not know. I know I am being negative, but I can't help but feel hopeless. In my whole life, up to just a few months ago, I have been in charge of what I want to do and where I end up. Nothing is possible being in here.

How can I be patient when I am subjected to such hostile conditions? How can anyone possibly be sane when they are being told when to eat, watched when you have to urinate, have a lights-out, and have a snack time? It is like being a three-year-old again.

I have been very sick today. I think it is all the medicine they give me. The doctor keeps switching the pills to see what works. I know it must be hard on my stomach. I have been throwing up all day. I blacked out again, so I had to go back to my room and rest. At least the ward is pretty quiet right now. Patty is sleeping on the couch. Shelly Ann is, as always, guarding the phone. I try to stay away from her because I start yelling at her and we get in trouble from the nurses. She makes me so mad, she gives me headaches.

I am hoping for a hall pass today. I am so tired of not being able to go outside. It would be great if I could just go back to Yosemite—out in the open fresh air with streams and mountains! A good run through the foothills would be a real treat. It seems like an eternity since the last time I ran. I guess that would have been up in Idaho. I wonder if I will ever run again, whether for another school or even my own pleasure.

(Later . . .) Well, it turns out that I didn't get a hall pass. I was sick the rest of the day. I just threw up trying to brush my teeth. Now we are being told to turn off the lights. I am so miserable. I want out so bad. I want to break everything in sight so I can run away. When I look out my barred window, I see my life just passing me by. I wonder if I will ever be happy again and enjoy that world out there.

NOTE: Medication for psychological illness is still as much an art as a science. Undeniably, the medication is necessary, but the psychosomatic chemistry and processes of the human makeup are extremely complex, and so it does take trial and error, and sometimes inspiration, to get the type of medicine and the dosage right. This period of adjustment is seldom pleasant for the patient, but when the right combination is established, the patient experiences herself as much more able to cope with and succeed in human society than they have been previously. On the other hand, manic symptoms do include feelings on the patient's part that she knows more than the attending physicians and nurses and, hence, often includes a delusion on the patient's part that he or she is a guru or messiah figure for fellow patients. (This information is from direct observation of several cases involving psychotropic drugs, pharmacological papers presented on the Web sites lib.bioinfo.pl, psychosomaticmedicine.org, bipolarinfo.com, and conversations with clinical psychologists.)

Chapter 21

LOCKDOWN

Today is just too awful. It is hard to write. The white coats took all the patients, except me, to the open ward. I am all by myself.

I was trying to help everybody with his or her problems. The doctor said I was wearing myself out playing the psychiatrist. Basically, I was just trying to get them out quick before they get stuck in here like me. I know it was working too because I got a lady out almost right away! I bet I could do better jobs than the doctors here anyway.

The patients even said they liked my therapy concepts better than the docs'. It is extremely quiet and lonely now that there is nobody over on this side of the ward. Having none of the usual sounds is strange.

Plus, the radio and TV are off-limits to me, and I am all done with the puzzle Amy gave me. I really have nothing to do or write about.

I followed every single rule today since there was nothing else to occupy my concentration. The nurse finally gave me a hall pass! It was my first time outside in about a week or so. It felt so good to soak up the sunshine and breathe the fresh air. Mom, Dad, and Tom took me out to the Diamondback Café, my favorite lunch spot. I had a salad with the house dressing, the best fries ever, and a chicken teriyaki sandwich—oh, and a pickle! It was the best lunch of my entire life. I ran up and down Main Street screaming with joy as Tom ran after me! I just needed to take in all the smells before I had to go back to the terrible, smothering hole. Mom took me into the Princess Shop, which has been my favorite shop since I was a little girl. A beautiful woman named Patricia owns it, and she is so kind to me.

Back at the hospital, I am once again all by myself. There was a patient here a short time ago named Tim. I told him every step of what to do to get out of here.

He did everything I told him and was out of here by four o'clock this afternoon.

I also had told him to stop by Dad's ranch to get a job. I have been following all the rules and then some, but it does not seem to faze the nurses and doctors.

Right now, I am just staring at all the Nurse Ratcheds on the other side of the glass. They sit there with their clipboards and observe me. I feel as though I am on exhibit at the zoo.

I can see the patients on the other side of the ward. They are all watching a movie and laughing. This makes me feel pretty bad and a little angry. They all get to go outside for ten minutes every hour.

(Later . . .) I got so bored, I decided to give the nurses a little action. When my food tray came, I threw it as hard as I could against the glass. I found this very funny. The Ratcheds, however, were thrown into quite a stir. I was sent to my room with no food. Oh well, it was ever so worth it!

Chapter 22

SUNFLOWERS

Journal Entry - May 10, 1996

I just got back from seeing the doctor. I don't think she has a clue what to do with me or what my diagnosis is. I have asked several times for my diagnosis, but she will not tell me. Today, I got so bored that I rubbed sunflower pollen all over my face and went running up and down the hall screaming at the nurses. I thought, Why not do this, since I am in a mental hospital? If they want to see crazy, I'll show them crazy! Then I started shouting Little Mermaid songs as loud as I could until the nurses just about lost it. I was making all of them go nuts! I enjoyed making trouble for them too. I wanted them to feel my pain and anguish for having nothing to do in this nasty place. I don't even want to write anymore today because I am so enraged!

Journal Entry - May 11, 1996

Today I started reading something very interesting. It just may be my ticket to freedom. It is the Patient's Handbook on Your Rights. I am writing an entire list of how the Nurse Ratcheds have wronged me. It says in here that I can even have a rights advocate to assist me if my rights have been taken away. I have already yelled at one nurse to back off, or I was going to report her to my lawyer. I'm going to take this whole hospital down! This place won't know what hit them when I release my venom. If it sounds like I am getting all fired up, well, I am! This place needs to be shown how awful they treat their patients. I am still all by myself and am angry as all get out!

Chapter 23

MANIC

Journal Entry - May 12, 1996

Today, I got to speak with my advocate. The woman said she would set up some kind of meeting with my family, my doctors, and my counselor, Kate. My moods are so bad I can't control them anymore. This morning, I put on my shoes and kicked a hole in the wall. The nurse told me if I did not calm down, they would put restraints on me. That sobered me up pretty quick. I really don't want to go into that room where they took Steve. I hope the meeting with everybody will come soon. I personally think it is the hospital, not anything wrong with myself, that is giving me these horrible moods.

I remember one nurse calling me manic. What on earth is that? Whatever it is, I am not that. I should have put a fist through her face for saying that! She is not the doctor anyway, so there is nothing to worry about, right? I hope so. I just want to get out of here now!

Chapter 24

JULIE

Today I got my meeting, so I can work on leaving. The doctor said I am here on a fourteen-day hold, and I cannot leave until the fourteen days are up. If that's the case, I still have two to three days left in this joint. Of course, I am still all by myself. It is so dull in here as I watch the clock slow down to a snail crawl. I'm going completely nuts due to boredom. My anger is out of control and so are my actions. There is nothing I can do to stop myself. For now, though, I am going to try to sleep a little on the couch.

After my nap, the nurse said I could have one hour with the other patients in their TV room. It was so nice to talk to the others.

Most of the patients that I had known had all been released. I did meet an extremely wonderful woman named Julie. I swear she is my soul sister. She and I are a lot alike and feel the same way about tons of topics. Both of us play the piano, and the nurse let us play one together. It is definitely the best time I have had since I have been here.

Amy's View - The Bad Time

I continued to come home when my job allowed, but I never knew what I would find. Maggie's reality was pure fantasy. She seemed to be possessed.

Then she was hospitalized the first time, and for the first time, we had a name for what was happening—manic depression. Excuse me? My sister has a mental illness? And then they called and said to come and pick her up! I remember looking at my mom and saying, "You mean now that we know what is wrong, she is cured?" Apparently not so fast—they just taught her how to sign her own release papers! I have always wondered how the person responsible for that deed sleeps at night. Maggie looked horrible. Her eyes were wide and seemed to have black circles around them. She was still existing on about two hours of sleep at night. Like a robot, she would shut down at 2:00 a.m. and start up at 4:00 a.m., and then for the next twenty-two hours, she was on the run. And those twenty-two hours were hell for the rest of us.

Everything she did was inappropriate—her language, behavior, the way she looked and even dressed. It seemed as if everybody in our family was yelling at everybody else, and no one was getting a break at all! I finally realized I needed help for me, so I went to a counselor at my company. The idea that manic depression was an illness finally began to sink in. She was sick—only not in her body, but also in her head. My counselor gave me tools to help me deal with her, and I learned to set boundaries for myself.

For instance, I just couldn't stand for her to yell "fuck you" at me—that language just made me sick, so I would walk away, with her still yelling. But she needed someone to yell at, so she would follow me, and finally get it—that I would listen or stay, but the language had to be cleaned up. Small victories— but mine! The last thing you want to do is say the wrong thing. It's a little like a boxing match—you are in the ring, but your arms are tied behind your back.

You are getting hit—right and left—and boy, do you have an awesome left hook ready, but you can't use it! What if that one hit pushes her off the cliff? The tightrope our family was walking got tighter and tighter.

Chapter 25

DR. H.

I don't know how many more days I was in the hospital before I was released.

I do know I was there a total of fourteen days. I also remember the meeting about my release. I didn't write in my journal for over a week. When I was back on the outside, my mind kept spinning more out of control by the day. I had to take high doses of lithium to control my mood swings. I was now seeing a doctor in Modesto named Dr. H. He was a tall thin man with little round wire glasses that rested on a long pointy nose. He had a thick Polish accent. For me, our appointments were like visiting Dr. Death. I didn't like him: the large doses of lithium he was giving me made me very ill. I had projectile vomiting five or six times a day.

It took weeks for Dr. H. to realize that the lithium doses were too high and were poisoning my system. Mom called him frequently to tell him how much I was throwing up the medicine. Even worse, the lithium wasn't calming my mood; it merely made me sick, very thirsty, and drowsy all day. I had stopped writing my journal for a while, and I don't remember much of what I did then.

NOTE: Lithium, in several forms, is a standard prescription for bipolar disorder. However, it also has the drawback of having to be carefully monitored as lithium overdose can cause renal failure. In a report published by pharmacologists Sean Patrick Nordt, PharmD, and F. Lee Cantrell, PharmD, on the Web site psychosomaticmedicine.com, symptoms of lithium overdose poisoning were given as severe frequent vomiting, tremors, and frequent drowsiness. It could be surmised that, even at this early stage in Maggie's treatment for mania, she was receiving too much lithium. In cases like this, the prescribing doctor would normally monitor the patient's symptoms and perhaps would prescribe a different form of lithium as this particular prescription was apparently both ineffective and was prescribed to be administered at such high levels as to be poisonous.

Chapter 26

BIPOLAR DISORDER

Journal Entry - May 27, 1996

I have not written in my journal since my hospitalization, but I finally have my big diagnosis. The doctors are telling me that I am manic-depressive or the newer term, bipolar disorder. I am very relieved that I have an actual, identifiable condition. It was hard to have everybody call me sick when I didn't know what my sickness was. I guess my illness is defined as being alternately severely depressed or wild, crazy, and out of control. It seems weird that I, Maggie Hurst, have a chemical imbalance. What did I do to deserve this? It feels like I am being punished for no reason. The doctor said I was born with this disorder. I guess it comes out later in your life in a time of crisis. My downfall was when my running career came to an end. Anyway, the news is still confusing. The doctors say I have to be on medication for the rest of my life, in combination with therapy, and blood workups to check for kidney damage. This is all a lot to take in right now.

Right this minute, I feel fine and in control of myself. Is this illness real, or is it some kind of hoax? I always thought that mental illness was something that people cause themselves. I guess I was wrong.

Since I got out of the hospital, I have had two huge out-of-control manic attacks. I don't know what else to call them. There are these times when my brain just goes nuts. It feels like I cannot do anything to control my actions.

Anyway, this is what happened: I went over to Dani's house. She said I was being too crazy and kicked me out. She was the one smoking pot anyway. I was so mad at being kicked out that I just started running down the street, and then Dad showed up in his pickup. Dad jumped out of the truck and tried to catch me. This just made me run faster. I was running across streets without looking for traffic, and shouting at anyone I saw.

I ended up across town out of breath, with Dad hanging on to me. Two elderly women in a car slammed on their brakes, thinking that Dad was a stranger trying to hurt me. Dad must have told them I was sick, and that we needed a ride back to his truck, because the next thing I knew, we were in the truck, driving back home. Every time I have tried to get away from Dad, he has been one step ahead of me. It is as if he knows my thinking. Anyhow, I was so angry at Dad that I wanted to jump out onto the side of the road. The last thing I wanted to hear was Dad saying to me, "Maggie, you're not well, and you need more help." I think everyone else should get a little therapy. All I want is my life back.

Is that too much to ask?

Chapter 27

TWISTER

It is hard to say exactly how many days later I wrote the following entry, but it was probably around late May 1996. By this time, the mania had taken over severely, and it was then impossible for me to even know what day of the week it was. I was not functioning well, and I knew it. This was an extremely frustrating time.

Sometime later . . .

I would write the date if I knew it, but I have lost track of time.

Days turn into nights, and long nights turn into even longer days.

Tonight, I got into more trouble. I don't mean to get into situations.

They just happen. Mom and Dad took me to some stupid movie called Twister. The movie was just as I expected, slow and boring. I was ready to go within fifteen minutes of the show starting. What I really wanted was to get some fresh air, so I told Mom and Dad that I needed to go to the bathroom. Actually, I was on my way out of the theater when I saw a group of college-age guys getting popcorn.

They asked me where the Frogtown Fair was and wanted to know if I would take them there. Just as I left the theater with them, Dad came bolting through the door and caused a huge scene. Well, after that, the night out was over. Mom, Dad, and I left immediately, and I was insanely angry!

Chapter 28

HUNTINGTON BEACH

Soon after the Twister fiasco, Dad decided that I needed to get out of town for a few days and go to Los Angeles to visit my grandparents. I recorded my thoughts about this trip in the following undated journal entry that happened in early June 1996.

Dad was so kind. He took me to Los Angeles for the weekend.

We had so much fun. We stayed at the Hampton Hotel in West Covina. There, I was able to see my grandparents and aunt. We also went to Huntington Beach for a day trip. I asked a nice girl named Claire, who worked at the Hampton, if she would like to come along.

A major aspect of my mania was socializing with complete strangers. I could talk to anyone. I felt that everyone was my friend. My journal is filled with countless names and numbers of people that I talked with and don't know.

Claire was one of them.

She took the day off and came with us. We had the best time! It seemed like I had known her all my life. The only part of the trip that bothered me was the way my grandfather looked at me with such worry on his face. (I hope he lasts forever. He is such a wonderful grandpa.) My cousin looked at me as if I had totally gone nuts. I feel fine, that's the strange part. When everybody looks at you like you're crazy, it really starts to put the doubt in your head.

After we got back from the LA trip, home was not getting any easier for any of us. Everyone was completely stressed out. Every morning, my mother would plead with me to take my lithium, and I would always put up a fuss about it. She bought me a pill case, like the ones old people use, with each day of the week labeled in a separate compartment for each pill. This was supposed to make my taking my medications easier, but instead, it just made me angry.. I was angry about taking the pills, and I would throw them in a fit of rage.

My parents were overwhelmed, and they hired one of my old high school friends to take me around during the day. Josh was expected to make sure I stayed out of trouble, took my medications, and ate some food too. This would be a tall order for anyone with psychiatric training, much less a nineteen-year old on summer break. The first few days went well for me. For Josh, though, it was tough. I had no idea how much trouble I made for him. After four days, he told my parents that the job was too much, and he quit. Looking back, I can't blame him, as I was almost uncontrollable.

Around the first week of June 1996 Josh quit being my bodyguard. He says he is too stressed out to keep up with me, whatever that means! I guess he is scared of me too.

Carrie is also not putting up with me—my best friend, of all people, is pretty much leaving me for the vultures. Everyone is against me! My own dad and brother restrained me on the couch because they thought I was going to hurt somebody. It makes me extremely sad and angry to think that my family would see me as a killer. Killer? Nonsense! I wouldn't hurt a flea.

NOTE: When a bipolar sufferer is caught deep within their cycle, both the manic and the depressive states are psychologically myopic, like Mr. Magoo, persons trapped at either end of the mood spectrum cannot see much beyond themselves. Even at that, what they perceive is distorted by the powerful brain-chemical changes that are hurling them either into the dark abyss of despair or into the blinding hot sunlight of self-aggrandizing fantasies. In either case, the patient feels as if the world in some way reflects his or her own inner feelings when in fact the world seldom does. Hence, it is difficult for such a patient to understand, in any realistic fashion, how others are affected by their actions. Thus, it is important for those near them, caregivers, family, and friends, to help them assess their state and to have an understanding that others care for them. It is important that they know they are not alone and, at the same time, that others are there to help them find the acceptable limits of their behavior. (Understandings gleaned from Hurst family notes and documents, the autobiography Girl, Interrupted, the Web site bipolar.com, and personal discussions with clinical psychologists.)

Chapter 29

JENNY

Mom and Dad's next idea was to give me something to occupy my time, give me a little responsibility and direction. A puppy would be the perfect fit. We decided to look for a dog. I wanted a bullmastiff, but my parents talked me into looking for a Labrador retriever.

Undated (probably early June 1996) I bought a beautiful yellow Labrador for $600. Mom and Dad paid half for her! Mom said I would have a lot of responsibility in taking care of the new puppy. I think I will name her Jenny Three Toes. She really does have three toes on her back foot! Yesterday, I went to Modesto to Dr. H. I really hate going there; in fact, I really hate him! He told me that I probably would not have any children.

Where does he get off telling me that? I can have kids if I want; it is my life, not his. I didn't like anything he had to say. He just kept crushing every idea I came up with, saying none of it was based in reality. That word reality is really starting to get on my nerves.

Today I talked to a couple of guys from Yosemite. They sounded great and wanted to know if I was ever coming back. I never wanted to leave that beautiful place. It was the stupid park rangers that made me leave. I can't even remember the reason for leaving. I know I didn't do anything wrong. I guess that doctor thought I was some kind of threat! That seems very funny to me that anyone could think that I was a threat. What's the deal with all the adults trying to rule my life anyway? I thought when you turned eighteen, you were in charge—not your parents, not doctors, not anyone but yourself. So why is everyone after me? It is as if they are all after my wonderful plans and want to take my great ideas for themselves. Or maybe they would all like to have my many talents. I know that if I want to, I can go to the top of any field I choose if I put my mind to it. I have always had to be the best at whatever really interests me: from summer camps to acting camps to running and other sports, I always came out on top. Now I even want to go further with my talents, and everyone just wants to shut me down by saying I am sick. Maybe once in a while, things don't seem the same as last year. However, that happens to everyone. You change and want to try new things! I really don't want to do all the academic college crap stuff anyway.

Mom and Dad thought that Jenny was a way to slow me down a little. They hoped that I would care enough about the little puppy that perhaps I would start caring about my own health and start taking my illness seriously. At first, I was really into little Jenny. That was very short-lived, though, due to my head spinning out of control. I feel sad when I think about everything my family tried to do to get me well.

You have no idea how amazing your family and friends can be in times of crisis! Then again, there are some who don't have that support, and you see them wandering the streets, abusing drugs or alcohol to numb the pain, and some are runaways never to be found again. Many of them are bipolar or have another mental illness. I wish for the world I could save them all. Wouldn't it be wonderful if we could all find that "happy" pill to make us well, to let us function normally? I was lucky; I had the support necessary to get me through the mess I was in, however ugly it became.

NOTE: The Mayo Clinic cites that in Bipolar I disorder, the patient has had "at least one manic episode, with or without previous episodes of depression," while Bipolar II disorder involves a long phase of depression and shorter relatively light phases of mania (referred to as hypomania, meaning "lesser mania") that enable the patient to function almost normally without hospitalization. The mania portion of Bipolar I disorder is more intense and debilitating. As the Web site goes on to explain: "Severe episodes of either mania or depression may result in psychosis, or a detachment from reality. Symptoms of psychosis may include hearing or seeing things that aren't there (hallucinations) and false but strongly held beliefs (delusions)" (from http://www.mayoclinic.com/health/bipolar-disorder/DS00356/DSECTION=symptoms)

Chapter 30

THREAT

Journal Entry – A couple days have gone by.

I just had another manic episode. I swore at Dad and threatened my mom's life. I didn't mean it. All I was trying to do was have a fun night with my friends Alyssa and Cammie. Alyssa called me up and said they were going out and wanted to know if I could go.

It's not as if I was going to go out and party or anything. Anyway, Mom and Dad said no, and that's when the incredible manic rage came out of me. I don't know why I get like this. I never got mad at my parents when I was growing up, so why am I now blowing up like gunpowder? My anger gets so incredibly intense it hurts my head, and everything inside me feels toxic. Sometimes things are moving so fast it is like a blur of rushing me at warp speed. What is happening to my mind? Am I going insane like everyone says? Am I really crazy? On our property by the creek, we have Indian grinding bowls—craters in the rocks made in the nineteenth century and earlier by local tribeswomen grinding acorns and grains into powder for food. I scared my friends when I told them I was seeing Indians grinding flour there, where there hadn't been Indians for many years.

Did I really see those Indians at the creek, or was it all in my head? And what about the man I saw sitting on our spiked fence, and Ju said there was nothing there and ran off screaming? What is going on? So many questions with nobody to answer them. Would somebody please tell me? Mom looks at me with fright and worry, Dad seems like he is trying to cage me like an animal, Amy is scared of me, and Tom sees me as a sister he doesn't know anymore. I am afraid of myself and my mind. Is this what madness is really like?

Chapter 31

THE WEDDING

As the mania continued, my parents kept hoping and praying that the medications would take hold and slow me down. In the meantime, I was on a short leash. My cousin was getting married, and I badly wanted to go to the wedding with the rest of my family. We drove to Fresno and spent the night in a hotel.

Journal Entry - June 11, 1996

My cousin was married earlier today. I was not allowed to go to the wedding. I had to stay in the hotel with Dad. Boy, that really made me mad! Everything is being taken away from me! I am so furious right now, I just want to blow up into a million pieces. I feel like I am hearing voices in my head. I know it is that lousy medicine.

Those stupid visions are probably from that stuff too. If the doctors would just let me be, I know I would be fine. I am definitely not going to tell my doc about any voices or visions! If I did, he would put me in some state ward, lock me up, and throw away the key. I am so angry! When I would fly into these rages, it was unstoppable. I could not clear my head and calm down even if I wanted to. The anger was so intense it seemed as though my veins would pop out of my body. I remember that when I was like this, I would try to stop myself, but it was impossible. The mood swings were so powerful that it was as if I were suddenly possessed by an evil demon.

Then when the anger subsided, my body felt weak, and my hands were cold and clammy. These were terrible ordeals to go through.

The scariest part of these rages was that no one knew what would set me off. One thing that always put me into a full rage was being hot. One day, my parents took me to a beautiful mountain lake named Pinecrest. The day went fairly smoothly until I met up with a bunch of college-age guys. They asked if I wanted a ride in their boat. My parents were not there at the moment, and I decided it would be fun to go with them. I had a great time yelling and screaming like a wild woman as we zipped along in their boat. I remember having on a broad-brimmed hat that I had impulsively bought for too much money. The guys got really wild and spun the boat in fast, tight circles; I lost my balance and went overboard! I swallowed a lot of water, my hat was ruined, I was soaking wet, and the rage hit me like the blazing heat from an incinerator. As the guys pulled me into the boat, I screamed insults at them, "You fucking assholes, get me back to the shore now!" They were astonished by the frightening intensity of my anger. They were speechless and immediately sped toward the shoreline.

Back on the beach, Dad spotted me. He had been looking all over for me, and now, he sprinted toward me. He was really angry that I took off without telling him where I had gone. He and Mom immediately packed everything up, and we were off for home. On the way, I asked for some water. I was dehydrated from our time in the sun, forgetting to drink anything all day, plus the lithium gave me cotton mouth. Mom decided we would stop off at KFC for dinner and to get me some water. The plan seemed simple enough until we got there. As we pulled into the drive-through, I started to panic.

"Dad, get me some water, quick!" I shrieked, in hysterics in the back seat.

"Margaret, calm down," he soothed, "we're almost through this line. You'll have water in less than a minute." As we pulled forward to the pickup window and began bringing our order through the window, I couldn't take it anymore.

"Get me some fucking water now!" Then I told my dad that if he didn't get me my water, I was going to tell the lady in the window that he was molesting me! Suddenly ice-cold water splashed all over my face and down my shirt, completely soaking me from the head down to my waist. Mom had thrown my cup of water all over me. I was completely shocked! It shut me up right away though, and we rode home in a cold, wet silence.

Chapter 32

MEDICATIONS

Journal Entry - June 13, 1996

Things are going much better. I am not so manic lately. The medicine really makes me sick though. I have been throwing up five or six times a day, and it shoots out of my mouth like a fire hose.

It's disgusting! The medicine I am on is called lithium. It makes me extremely thirsty. It also makes me drowsy, and my hands shake quite a bit. I also really look like a mess. I hate this drug. It is sucking the life out of me. It is making me so sick, Mom is trying to get the doctor to put me on a new medication.

I think that Dr. H. has no idea what patients go through on this medication. You know what I would do if I were in charge? I would make the doctor take the meds. See how he feels being sedated all the time. I feel like one of those animals on the Discovery Channel that gets shot with a tranquilizer dart, and then the scientists come and analyze and poke me with prods. The world is so unjust.

I forgot to say that Tom graduated high school. I didn't see much of the ceremony because I couldn't sit down. My head was going too fast. I don't know why it speeds up like that, but it hurts my entire body. I feel myself racing inside, and it gets faster and faster. There is nothing I can do but get out and run wild to release that crazy energy.

(When Josh was my bodyguard, he tried to keep up with my talking and my physical speed. But I was way too smart for him and can outthink him ten times.) The last few nights, Julie, my manic friend that I met on the psych ward, has picked me up. We usually head up to sing karaoke at the Sonora Inn. My favorite song to sing with Julie is Patsy Cline's "Crazy." When I sing that song, I feel like I am talking about myself and trying to make everyone understand what is happening to me.

When Julie and I are not singing, we always go to the coffee shop downtown and have decaf mochas. Julie says it is not good for us to have caffeine, so I follow suit. While we sit and sip our drinks, we talk about travel and becoming famous with our singing and other plans. We are well suited for each other as far as friends go. Even though she is twelve years older, we think alike, act alike, and have the same aspirations in life. Julie has even made some of her own music, including one song I just love, which goes, "I'm not the city girl I used to be, I've known lately that there's country in me." Julie is so special! She shouldn't have to go through the pain of having this awful illness that we both endure.

Julie was a real eye-opener for me. She had been diagnosed with bipolar disorder at the age of twenty. Here she was thirty-one, in and out of the psych ward, living on disability. That scared me. I don't remember too much of what she told me about her twenties, but I know that was a terribly hard time for her.

She had lived in San Francisco then, selling shoes and playing the piano. From what I gathered, she had been very successful at both. She could sell shoes to any customer that would come to her. As for the piano, she played endless hours beautifully without any sheet music. That is one interesting thing about being bipolar; it seems that many successful people have suffered from this illness— Carrie Fisher, Ed Bradley, and even Van Gogh are a few examples of this.

Julie had been hospitalized a number of times in the city before her family moved her out of the city's frenetic pace (which manic energy feeds on) to the country. In Jamestown, the illness continued to control her life, and she ended up back in the psych ward and on full disability. When I met her, she was trying to get back on track once again, after a manic episode. When I met her family, I could tell they had been worn down by Julie's illness.

Bipolar disorder is a horrible illness. Obviously, it is extremely hard on the people that suffer from it, but I think it is equally hard for the families and friends who are trying to help their loved one regain control of their life.

Chapter 33

NUTS

My manic-bipolar shit is getting better. It is so strange to know that I have some kind of chemical imbalance. Sometimes I do kind of believe everyone and think that there really is a problem with my head, but then other times, I feel completely fine and feel that everyone else is nuts. I don't know; things are too confusing right now. I don't know what to think. I could describe the episodes, but they are so overpowering it seems like there is not an easy way to tell what they are like. The different moods I go through are so intense.

When I am up, it seems like I am floating outside my body. I feel like I am in control of everything and everyone around me. It is as if I am on some happiness drug that nobody else can have. People ask me where they can get the drug, but I tell them I generate my own drugs.

They cannot have it, and it cannot be bought! I would give anything to not have whatever this is when the anger rolls in. It is like a dark storm cloud with lightning bolts striking down into the earth. It is a storm that nobody can take cover from if they're in its path. When the anger is upon me, I feel that whoever is in my way, I will strike down and hurt. Then I remember later what I had thought and done, and feel awful.

Journal Entry - June 15, 1996

Since Josh quit, I have no one to take me around. I am very upset and ready to just die. I am tired of being this way. I am tired of running around all night with no sleep. I just want my life back.

With Josh gone, I cannot leave our property during the day. All the car keys are hidden. The phones are unplugged so I can't call my friends. I cannot leave without Dad tracking me down. He comes up from the store about every five minutes it seems. The only thing I am looking forward to is Julie picking me up tonight to go to karaoke.

I have been invited to go water-skiing tomorrow with my old friend Todd, whom I have known since grade school. Mom says if I keep taking my medicine and follow some simple rules, I can go. So I am really trying to hold back my manic thoughts and urges. I don't know if I can even get up on skis like I used to, but I'll sure try.

Anything is better than being stuck in this old garage. Oh, I probably didn't write anything about it earlier, but I moved out of the house and into the garage. I was tired of being in the house. I moved a roll-away bed out there and set up a card table and chairs. I have the only key and the door opener so my parents cannot get in.

Plus, if I feel like leaving at night for a walk, I can do it without them knowing. That's where I am now in fact. You should see my place! I have covered the wall with magazine pictures of models and colorful clippings glued everywhere. I have pasted hundreds of magazine pages all over it. Then I poured a couple bottles of glue over the tabletop and painted it on. Now the table has a glossy top that looks fabulous.

The garage was quite a scene. If a normal person walked in, they could tell something was not right immediately. With all kinds of stuff thrown everywhere, articles glued to the walls, and books piled high with tons of marks in them, it was anything but normal. In fact, it was probably rather scary for anyone who came into that dark hole. Just thinking about how I lived makes me squeamish.

My appearance was totally changed from when I was depressed. I had my hair cut short, got a wavy perm, and lost twenty-five pounds. I went from a size 10 to a 4. It was crazy, so to speak. My eyes had a weird haze to them due to the meds and lack of sleep. I lost a lot of weight because I never wanted to eat.

My clothing style was even different. I would purposely hike my skirts up and wear tight pants and go braless and wear low-cut tank tops because I thought it was sexy. My mannerisms were very provocative. If I thought a guy was cute, I would just run right up to him and tell him so. I also wore makeup, which is something I never did before.

At night, I did the most dangerous things. After the lights went out in my parents' house, I pretended that I was on a mission. I would dress like a man for my adventure because I thought if I wore jeans, a baseball cap, and a baggy shirt, I could pass for a young man, which would be safer for a girl going out into the world by herself after dark. I also packed a dress and some shoes in a backpack, to change into when I arrived at my destination.

Then I set out through the night. I thought that if I walked along the highway, it would be dangerous, so I hopped fences and kept low to the ground, out of sight. I traveled the two miles on foot to Jamestown. There, I would find a decent-looking person and hitch a ride for the five-mile trip to Sonora, because Sonora offers more nightlife than Jamestown.

Then I would go directly to the Sonora Inn, enter the bathroom there, and change into my dress and nice shoes—my singing costume. The Sonora Inn's bar area, where the karaoke took place, was for those twenty-one and over.

With my sexy little skirts and flirtatiousness, I never had a problem getting in.

Then I would sign myself up for my songs: "Crazy" by Patsy Cline or "Sweet Dreams" by the Eurythmics. Because the lithium made me extremely thirsty, I would drink water all night long. After the bar closed for the night, I would call a cab or sometimes find someone I knew or had met to drop me off back home.

I thank God to this day that I was never picked up by a rapist or killer.

Chapter 34

MEETING MATT

On the day I was to go water-skiing with my old friend Todd, I walked in the house and was immediately transfixed by the sight of Todd's brother, Matt Reese. He was very physically fit, tall, extremely handsome, with blue eyes, long eyelashes, and had a beauty mark under his left eye.

"Hi, Matt," I said loudly. "Do you remember me?" "Maggie, it's good to see you. It's been a long time," he replied.

We had gone to school together for two years in grade school. He had been two grades ahead of me. Matt had also picked me first to be on his intramural basketball team. I remember that I had a crush on him when I was in seventh grade. He had been the cool older ninth grader that was the king of our little private school. Sure, I had my junior high boyfriends, but I always had thought Matt could not be beaten.

I started babbling to him about my recent life and that my parents were looking for a bodyguard for me since the last one had quit. I ended by saying, "Matt, you should come work for them. We could have a lot of fun together! All you have to do is drive me around and take me to lunch and the lake! My parents will pay you well, I promise you that." I don't know what Matt thought of all my fast talking, but I could tell he was interested. He was home for the summer, extremely bored, and needed some kind of summer job.

"Maggie, why don't you talk to your parents first and then give me a call," he said. I barely heard this because my mind was going about a hundred miles per hour. I saw there was a hot tub outside and suggested we go in.

He said, "Go ahead, Maggie, I will come out in a minute." I immediately jumped in and called out to him, "Come on, Matt, don't be shy. Let's have some fun!" Matt didn't get in after all, but sat there by the side of the tub, and we caught up on each other's lives.

After I got home later that night, I announced with the new-bodyguard proposal: "Mom, Dad, I have great news! I ran into Matt Reese today. He can help us out this summer." That is how I put my plan into action—to have Matt as my personal babysitter or bodyguard, as I liked to call him. Mom and Dad knew him from his being a fellow student of mine in elementary school and knew his parents as well. They also liked the fact that he had taken psychology in college. Mom believed that he was responsible as he was going into his senior year of college.

Mom and Dad called Matt later that night and hired him for $300 a week to come by every day and more or less babysit me.

"Matt, do you really know how sick Maggie is?" I heard my mother warn.

I guess Matt thought he could handle me because he showed up in his little Mazda sports car the next day. "I knew you couldn't say no to me," I said. "You have me to look after all day and even get paid. I hope you know how lucky you are!" I was infatuated with him.

Poor Matt was a little shell-shocked at my fast talk but brushed it off quickly so I wouldn't take too much notice. "Let's drive to Pinecrest," I shouted.

"It will be fabulous. I will go get my swimsuit and towel. Don't worry, you don't need anything, just yourself and your car." He insisted on talking to Mom before we went to make sure of where we were allowed to go and what his hours of watching me were. Matt went inside and discussed the details of the job with Mom for about an hour. Meanwhile, I had started doing projects in the garage. I was pasting dozens of magazine ads to a table, making a giant collage—which I thought was a real work of art.

I can't imagine what Matt thought when he came out to get me. I was blaring Madonna over my CD player while pouring Elmer's Glue over the table, trying to seal my artwork.

There were pictures of people and cutouts of words from magazines hanging up all over the garage. I had a mattress on the floor with clothes all over it.

There were weird collections of glass and other odd items lining the end of my mattress. In general, the place looked like it had been hit by a tornado. Matt was a bit surprised, but after a moment, we were off to Pinecrest. I think he was only beginning to see how sick I really was.

"I love my life," I screamed as I poked my head up through the open sunroof of his car and raised my hands high in the air. "Maggie, get down," Matt insisted. "You can't do that. You'll get hurt! And we could get a ticket. Please sit down and put your seat belt on, or we are going home." The "or we are going home" got my attention right away. I quickly squeezed myself back into the passenger-side bucket seat and crossed my arms.

"You're no fun, Matt." I pouted. "I need you to learn how to be more relaxed about rules and life in general." Matt said firmly, "Maggie, this is my first day with you, and we need to have an understanding. You can't do illegal things, or we'll both be in trouble." "Enough of all this lecturing," I said. "Now we are off to lake adventures.

"Let's rent a boat, sit on the beach, and trick as many people as we can!" "I don't even want to know," Matt replied.

At the lake, I was giddy as a schoolgirl. First, we got my beach bag and headed down to pick a spot by the water. I thought I looked like a movie star.

I wore a big white hat, a cute pink-and-white cover-up over my pink-and-black bikini, and my big, oversized sunglasses. I made Matt carry all the stuff and tried to walk like a fashion model.

"Come along, handsome," I teased.

Poor Matt just didn't know what to make of me as I sashayed and pranced and put on a real show for him and anyone else who cared.

"Matt, let's set up here," I said. Of course, it was right in the middle of the biggest crowd on the lakefront beach. I could tell that was the last place he wanted to be, but he was being generous and didn't want to spoil my fun.

"Matt, isn't this so much better than my home in Hollywood?" I said, hamming it up, and speaking loud enough for every one around us to hear. Matt gave me a puzzled look as I whispered in his ear, "Just pretend that I am famous and you are my bodyguard!" "Maggie, come on, don't be silly," he said under his breath. But I guess he was too tired to fight me on this one, so he eventually went along with my charade while we sat on the beach. I talked to him about all the movies I was going to be in when I "got back to Hollywood." Some people actually believed the ruse because Matt told me later that two women approached him on his way to the bathroom and wanted to know who's the actress he was with. When I grew tired of faking Hollywood tales, I suggested we go rent a speedboat. Mom and Dad gave Matt money for activities and food, so that was all taken care of.

"Come, darling," I cooed. "There are too many people that are way too close to me. I need some fresh air out on the lake." We decided to rent a speedboat for two hours and tour around the lake. The day was crystal clear with the sun pounding down on us.

"Maggie, you are something else indeed," Matt said. "Those people totally thought you were a movie star! I just can't believe it."

"Well, believe it," I said. "People will believe anything you say as long as you make yourself sound legit—people believe what they want to hear. Now they will have something to talk about. Pretty funny!" "Well, that was kind of funny but embarrassing too," Matt said. The wind on the lake felt good, but I began to get hot. With taking the medicine, I didn't do well in heat. Before Matt could do anything, I dove from the boat into the lake. I said, "Jump in, you cutie-pie. The water's really refreshing!" Matt got in, and I immediately swam up to him and grabbed him from behind. That startled him, and he said, "Maggie, you can't do that. I am on the job!" I said in a pouty voice, "Come on, Matt, loosen up a little, gosh." The rest of the day went on like this, with us splashing around in the water.

As we drove home, I didn't feel well because of the hot sun and the medication. "Matt, pull over right now," I said weakly. He did, and I threw up on the bushes by the side of the road.

"Don't worry, Matt," I said between heaves. "This is normal for me because of all the meds the doctor is making me take." Then I got back in the car and turned to Matt saying, "Do you think I am a maniac like they all say?" "Maggie, I don't know what to tell you—let's just take it one day at a time.

To me, you seem like a regular wild college girl." His response satisfied me greatly. At that moment, Matt was my angel.

Matt had put in a full day, and it was time for him to go home. I begged and pleaded with him to stay, but he protested that he needed his rest to prepare for tomorrow. So I reluctantly let him go home. Mom and Dad were pleased that they got a little time off from me and were glad that Matt had made it through the first day. I went on and on at dinner about how wonderful Matt was and what we were going to do the next day.

Matt had no idea that this was just the beginning of "adventures" with me. When we were together, I would do all sorts of wild things to get Matt to really notice me, because I wanted to be his girlfriend, not just the girl he was supposed to keep out of trouble. When I think back on our relationship at that time, I am sure that if Matt had not been so patient and kind and caring—had he been anyone else—he would have run screaming away from me in short order, but he did not.

Chapter 35

A NIGHT IN THE TOWN

Later that night, I decided to go to the Sonora Inn by what was then my usual method. I crossed the fence, walked through my neighbor's property, and then went down to the highway. My mind was racing as I began to walk up the road. I ducked into the bushes as cars drove by. I didn't want some crazy man to pull over and grab me. It took me about twenty-five minutes before I got to Jamestown where I usually hitched rides to Sonora. I was tired, but my mind was full of energy. Without thinking, I walked up to a lady who was coming out of the mini-mart and asked her for a ride. She said that would be fine but lectured me on how dangerous hitchhiking was. When she let me off in Sonora, she called out, "Don't you try that again, you hear me? Get a ride home from a friend!" At the Sonora Inn, I changed out of my hat and jeans and reapplied my makeup in the bathroom. I was going to have fun tonight singing karaoke. I went right over to the DJ and wrote my favorite songs on the list. I put down the songs "Crazy," "Just Another Manic Monday," and "Sweet Dreams (Are Made of This)." As I sat down at a table, I noticed an old classmate of mine. It was Darren from my cross-country team. Delighted, I made my way over to him. He was with his mom and a couple of other people.

"Maggie, it's great to see you," Darren said. "How are you allowed in the bar underage?" "Hey yourself," I said. "I come in here all the time and never get carded— maybe because I just order ice water. I guess you're okay to be here with your mom." "Yes, well, we decided to sing her a little song for her birthday," he said.

I sat with Darren, his friends, and his mom for the rest of the evening. I was only able to sing one of my songs before the night was over, but I didn't care; I was having fun catching up on news from Darren's freshman year at Cal Poly.

I got a ride home with him. As he dropped me off at the gate, he said, "Maggie, I hope you are doing okay. Just call me if you need anything." I walked up the dark driveway, thinking that he had sounded concerned and worried about my health. Why was everybody giving me the same runaround? Did he know I had been at the mental hospital? I couldn't help but think he must have heard a rumor about me. I put it out of my mind as the garage came into sight. I was extremely exhausted. It was about three in the morning. I flopped down on the mattress, hoping to get at least a little sleep. I lay there wide-awake but tired at the same time. I finally dozed off for about two hours.

Matt and me at the beach. (Courtesy of Mandi Wright)

Chapter 36

GOING PLACES WITH MATT

I awoke with a start about 6:00 a.m. My mind was back to warp speed again. I was still in the dress that I had worn the night before, and makeup was smeared all over me. I decided I should take a shower, especially since Matt would be coming over at eight. I usually didn't take time to clean myself up, but now that Matt was in the picture, I was focused on him. The hot water felt good on my body. As I washed my hair, I thought of Matt.

Right at eight, Matt rolled into the driveway. I did my hair up as cute as I could, and I put on some shorts and a tank top. Mom and Dad were off as soon as he walked in the door.

"Have a great day," my father said. "I will, Dad, thanks," I answered.

"So, Matt, what do you want to do today? Do you have any fun ideas?" "Yes, I do, in fact," he said. "I was thinking we could go over to my parents' house and relax, swim, do a little roller hockey, maybe some Ping-Pong. How does that sound?" "Sounds great," I said with excitement. "I love swimming, and I'll go get my Rollerblades. I will have to wear a brace though. I twisted my knee up really bad when I was working at Yosemite. Did I tell you that story?" Matt hadn't heard my Yosemite adventures, so I filled him in on the drive over to his house.

We had a great time swimming in his pool. I was able to bring little Jenny with me too. The Reeses also had a yellow Labrador named Watson. Matt's family were very fond of Labs and happy to have Jenny over for Watson's company. For our rollerblading hockey game, I brought over a little tight black Everlast sports bra with matching short spandex. I thought I looked so hot as I blasted around the pavement trying to score a goal on Matt.

After we were both tired, Matt made us some yummy smoothies. We took our drinks down to the lounge chairs by the pool and talked. I loved asking him about his past. He told funny stories about high school and college. I felt so comfortable spending time with him.

I was sure he liked me too, but he was on the job and couldn't let himself be caught up in any flirtation. Before he took me home, I begged him to take me to McDonald's for some fries. I always liked certain snacks, and this became quite our daily part of our routine—getting me my French fry fix! The next morning, I dressed in a really flattering dress and put on lots of makeup just for Matt. We were going to go to my doctor in Modesto. It would be an hour's drive, so I wanted to be extra attractive so Matt could get a good look at me. I was so excited as Matt came to pick me up. He did a double take at my outfit. Good, I thought to myself, my clothes are working! When we arrived in Modesto, we went to my doctor's office.

"Hi, Maggie," Dr. H. said. "How are you doing this week?" I shot back, "How are you doing this week, Dr. H.?" I loved bugging him this way. If he asked me a question, I would ask him the same back. Around and around we would go during our sessions.

"Maggie, if we are going to make progress, you can't answer everything I ask with a question," he said in a stern tone. "The sooner you start cooperating with me, the sooner you will get better." "Look, Doctor, I am better," I said in an annoyed way. "Why do you think I ask you questions? It's because this is boring! I feel fine, and I don't need you as doctor!" I tried to control myself, but I felt the anger taking me over. I knew by the tone of my voice that I had already lost control. I had wanted to stay calm this time to make him think he wasn't needed. My plan was falling apart, and falling apart fast. Just for once, I wanted to get through a session without losing it, but I couldn't. It was like there was a demon controlling my mouth, and I couldn't make it stop.

"Maggie, what did I say about using such language in my office! Let's not go down that road again. You get very worked up over simple visits with me, and that is getting us nowhere really fast. I see you are dressed differently this week. Is there a reason why you are dressing in a provocative way? How is your lithium working this week? I am getting the results of your blood workup in the morning. It will tell me if you are taking your meds like you are supposed to. "You want to hear about my medicine, I'll tell you about my fucking medicine," I yelled. By this time, my anger was so intense I felt as though I was a boiling pot of water. "That stuff you give me makes me insanely sick. I throw up like the Poltergeist girl, projectile vomiting and everything. You're killing me, you quack!" "Maggie, we cannot go on with the rest of this session. I will see you next week when you are in a calmer mood. Today we are not going to make any headway when you are this out of control," he said sharply.

As I got up to leave, I said between my teeth, "I didn't dress in a provocative way. I look great, you fucking piece of shit!" With that, I slammed the door and marched out to Matt, trying to regain my composure. I didn't want Matt to see me this way, so I stopped in the bathroom to straighten up a bit. I was so glad to be out of the doctor's office I forgot how mad I had been. Matt suggested we go out for lunch. We went to a little Mexican restaurant close by. I was in good spirits as we ordered, but then I got a little out of hand. For some reason, I couldn't stop laughing as we ordered. I was laughing so much Matt had to order for me.

He said, "Maggie, keep it down a little, people are staring at us!" "Oh, Matt," I laughed. "Ease up a bit and have a little fun." Instead of keeping it down, I began to get louder. Matt convinced me to quiet down after he threatened we would go home early if I didn't stop.

After lunch, as we were walking to the car, Matt got mad because I lit up a cigarette. I was in this weird smoking phase. It wasn't that I was addicted to cigarettes, but I liked them in my mouth for something to do. "Maggie, come on, you don't need those," he pleaded. "That's disgusting. You don't want to ruin your skin, do you?" I wished he hadn't said that—I couldn't smoke now that he said I had great skin and called me Maggie. I liked that, him calling me Maggie. I thought he might be falling in love with me! We decided to stop by the Modesto Mall on the way home. There we ran into some old friends from our school days so many years ago. I think they were a bit confused by the way I looked and why I was with Matt. I didn't care though. After walking through a few shops, I was bored and ready for the drive home.

The next few days were great. We would swim at his parents', play roller hockey, go get snacks around town, and relax by the pool. At the end of the week, Matt had to drop some things off for his brother, Todd. Todd was a summer camp counselor at a place called Leoni Meadows. I thought it would be a fun drive, so I wanted to go along. I brought my dog with us on the trip.

Jenny behaved like a good dog in the car and slept most of the ride. I began to get very sick again as we drove. We had to pull over about five different times while I threw up. Matt was extremely concerned, which comforted me greatly.

When we finally arrived at the summer camp, Todd was glad to see us.

"Maggie, Matt, thanks for coming," he said. "I need a break from all these campers! Let's go over to the counselor café and have a bite to eat." We followed Todd over to a cabin-like building and grabbed some lunch trays. Todd said it was fine to bring the puppy in since the supervisor was out for the day. As we ate lunch, Todd introduced us to his new friends. They all wanted to pet Jenny, which made me angry for some reason.

"Don't touch my dog," I snapped. Matt squeezed my leg and gave me a look that meant, "Be nice." I caught myself and said, "Sorry, but I don't like strangers petting her." After that, and for the remainder of the lunch, I tried to convince Todd's friends that I was visiting from Hollywood. I don't think I had a believer in the bunch, but it entertained me while Matt and Todd caught up with their family news. After lunch was over, we said our good-byes and were off to home again.

Matt and me in Hawaii. (Courtesy of Jim Reese)

Chapter 37

COURTING DISASTER

On Saturday and Sunday, it was hard to find things to do since Matt was off for the weekend. I tried doing more art projects in my garage room, became bored with it. Late on Saturday, I found a dead rattlesnake, which I thought was rather grand. I skinned the snake the best I could and nailed it to a long board. Then I used several different detergents on it, thinking they contained formaldehyde. I was proud of my work and took it up to the house to show Dad.

"Maggie, what are you doing with that rattlesnake?" he said incredulously.

I told him I found it dead and went on to say, "Doesn't it look great all pinned to the board? We could hang it up in your office if you want!" Dad didn't think too much of my idea and had me put it on the side of the garage until he could get rid of it on trash day. Later that night, Mom and Dad let me go to the Sonora Inn with my friend Julie from the hospital. Dad dropped us off and said he would be back at ten thirty to pick us up. I wanted to stay later, but Julie convinced me to agree. "Maggie, we are lucky to be going out at all," she whispered. I suppose she was right, but I still didn't have to like having a curfew at nineteen.

Julie and I always had a lot of fun together at the inn. We would pick songs to sing together and really get the crowd going. I told her there was nothing wrong with her, and she loved to hear that. She would say, "Maggie, when I am with you, I feel like I am a teenager again. You make me want to get more out of life, you make me laugh, and you are so kind." That night, while she was singing one of her favorite Judd songs, I decided to sit next to a cowboy. He turned to me and said, "Hey there, what's your name, sweetheart?" "Maggie," I replied. "And what might your name be, cowboy?" "Scott," he said in a flirtatious kind of way. We ended up talking for the rest of the night until Dad showed up to pick us up. Since in my frame of mind, people I met became instantly a friend, I decided to invite him to see my special swimming hole on the creek at the ranch. "Hey, Scott, if you want to come to my house tonight for a little fun, I left directions and a time where to meet later." I pushed a piece of folded paper into his pocket as I skipped outside to meet Dad.

Later that night, I sneaked down to the gate at about midnight. About five minutes later, the cowboy pulled in with a sly smile on his face. I had no idea who this man was and didn't care for that matter. He could have been some ax murderer for all I knew. That didn't even cross my mind: I had no reasoning power left in my warped brain. I jumped into his truck and told him to drive down the lane by the creek.

"I'll show you my special place," I said excitedly and made him turn off his headlights as we crept down the dirt road to the creek. The moon was full. "Hey, sweet thing," the cowboy slurred, "is there snakes down in these grasses?" He was slightly drunk.

"Ah, don't be such a baby," I said. "I killed one the other day with my bare hands!" I don't think he believed me, but I didn't care. I was on a mission to show him the swimming hole. "Look, there," I said in a hushed voice. "Isn't the pond beautiful in the moonlight?" The cowboy suggested we sit on the rocks and talk. Before long, he made it pretty clear that he didn't drive all the way down to Jamestown to look at the pretty moonlight on the creek! He tried to hug and kiss me, but I pushed him away.

I didn't like where this was going, but I couldn't figure a way out of it. He became increasingly more aggressive; suddenly I began talking my hyper-fast crazy talk, and that scared him. He hauled out of there in a flash.

I was extremely angry with myself for being so dumb. I made my way through the brush to my garage. Later that night, I ate some chicken and thought of Matt. I wished that he would take me away from all this craziness and that he could cure my fits of anger and then tell me that I'm fine. Even more than that, I wanted him to tell me that we would always be together.

Chapter 38

THE PROPER CHANNEL

Sunday went by in a blur. I was so glad it was already Monday. I missed Matt so much over the weekend. I looked out the driveway just as he pulled in. I ran out so quickly to meet him that I almost fell flat on my face.

"Matt, are you ready for another fun day with me? I thought we would go to White Bridges today and have a picnic lunch. Mom made us a lunch already!" "I've never been there," Matt said. "It sounds like a nice place to see." "It is," I said with a smile. "There are rocks to jump off, a waterfall, and pools everywhere. I have been there lots with Carrie. I hope there won't be too many people today—then we can have it all to ourselves!" White Bridges was a place teens liked to hang out. It was a very beautiful place with a river, pools, and a waterfall. I'd had so much fun over the years here. In high school, friends and I would go down the waterfall. It was the best place to swim in the summer, but it was hard trying to get down to the small sweet spot. We parked at the bridge by the side of the road. There was only one car already parked there; that was a good sign: no crowds today. The trail down to the river was steep and narrow. I saw that Matt was a bit nervous going down there.

"Don't worry, Matt," I teased. "Just take your time going down." We came to the edge of the cliff and looked down over one of the pools.

"Matt, this is the easiest way down. Just jump off the rock here. It's only about twenty-five feet or so!" "No way, Maggie," Matt said nervously. "There could be rocks under the water there. I'll take the side trail down and meet you down on that flat rock down there." "Fine, fine," I said. "You're really missing out though. This is the best jumping rock ever!" With that said, I jumped, yelling all the way down. I landed with a big splash.

I was still in my tennis shoes and clothes but didn't really care. Matt made his way carefully down the trail and set up on the hot flat rock. There wasn't a soul in sight! I swam over to Matt and lay out on the rock with a huge smile on my face. This was the life. I was sitting here with a gorgeous guy, overlooking a glorious stretch of water, and was about to eat a nice lunch. And there was no one but us to enjoy this wondrous place. As Matt laid out the blanket and lunch, I said, "So, Matt, tell me what you are going to be. Do you like college in Los Angeles?" "Yeah, I do," he said. "I am going to La Sierra University right now, finishing my major in physical education. I love that teachers have the summers off, and I love sports. So it seems like a perfect job for me. What do you want to do?" "Well, I have lots of plans," I said. "But first, I have to get my parents to let me go and live my life. Everyone keeps telling me that I am not well and that I can't go back to college until I get well. So I guess you could say I am in a holding pattern. Which I hate! But if I could go out and do what I want to, I would go to Hollywood and become an actress or maybe a singer. I am very talented in many areas, so it will be hard to choose what path I want to follow. I guarantee you, though, I will be somebody big. I just know it." Our conversation went on like this, flowing so easily that we might have known each other forever. I felt safe and secure, even normal, with him. He didn't make me feel like I was a mental case, and I loved that. We talked of our futures and our pasts, and even had quiet moments, taking in the amazing scenery around us. When we didn't talk, the silence was comfortable, and it made me want to be near him more than ever.

After we finished our lunch, I suggested that we hike up to the next pool.

It was a nice little spot that was very secluded. There were rocks all around the pool. I dove in, and Matt did too. Pretty soon, I felt something biting my legs. I asked Matt, "Do you feel something on you? I think we should get out of here." "Good idea," Matt hollered. As soon as we got back on dry land, I saw there were leeches on my legs. I started screaming as Matt ran over to me. He pulled them off me, and I did the same for him.

"Gosh, I didn't know there were leeches at this place," I said. "Thanks for taking them off me." Then I hugged him and gave him a kiss, and he didn't resist! Then we went for a nice swim in the water back by our lunches where there were no leeches. Later, in the car heading home, we decided to go back to his house. For the rest of the day, we relaxed by his parents' pool, feeling wonderful.

I know that, at first, Matt didn't want to have a romantic relationship with me; but now it seemed to be working out that way. Our days together just felt good. He was spending more time with me. I don't know if he wanted to or it was because I begged him to. We would drive to the lake a lot, go to his house, and go to White Bridges. One day, we got a boat and tied it to a tree at: a secluded spot on the far side of the lake. I gave him a kiss. I was enjoying myself more than usual that day, and before I knew it, it was time for Matt to take me home.

This moment in our times together always rattled me; I always got angry when it was time for him to take me home, as if he was leaving me forever. This time, I yelled at him in the car and tried to grab the wheel. He slammed on the brakes in the middle of the road.

"Maggie, please calm down, you know I have to take you home, and I have to go too," he said this in a calm voice.

"No, you don't," I cried. "Why can't you stay with me? I always show you a good time, don't I? Please don't go, Matt." I carried on this way until a police officer pulled up behind us. Matt put his head down on the steering wheel and muttered, "It's over now." I jumped out of the car and went over the cop. "Hi, Officer," I said calmly.

"We will be on our way, we didn't mean to stop in the middle of the road. We were discussing where to go. Sorry about that, sir." It was as I had turned on a switch. I had gone from very crazy to a normal, calm person. "You're sure everything is all right?" the officer said, glancing suspiciously toward Matt.

"Yes, thanks for asking." I smiled. I then got back into the car, and we were off. Matt said we would drive around for a little bit if I agreed that then he could leave. I decided that would be fine.

As the week went on, I became increasingly more confrontational when Matt's time was up. My anger was becoming more frequent, and I couldn't control it at all. One day, Matt's patience with my behavior ended. He decided just to leave whether I was going or not. I chased him down the lane, dripping wet from the lake, and pounding my fists on the car. Matt was scared out of his mind. He let me in the car and waited until I calmed down before we drove off together.

On another occasion, I thought it would be fun if he came with me to the Sonora Inn. I was so glad he was there with me that night. Suddenly, I noticed a lot of people there who seemed pretty rough and not exactly suitable for taking home to meet your family. They had probably always been there, yet in my often delusional state, I hadn't noticed them before Matt pointed them out.

"Maggie, you don't belong here with this crowd," he said. "Let's go home, relax, and watch a movie." "All right," I answered. "But first I want to sing my 'Crazy' song by Patsy Cline." We stayed until I sang my song, which I thought was fantastic. In reality, I wasn't a good singer, and Matt realized that quickly.

Back at the house, we watched a movie and ate popcorn. It was nice to actually be able to follow the plot and action of a movie. Usually I couldn't sit still for five minutes. This made me think about how sick I really was. If, normally, I could not sit still during a movie, what about everything else in life that was of a lot more importance? I just wanted to get well again so I could date Matt with no problems. Then I realized that I had to keep my love for Matt a secret until I did get better, and that was hard for me. I also realized, in that moment of clarity, that I had been treating my parents badly too. I decided to talk to Mom about trying a different medicine that might work better than the lithium. The high doses of lithium seemed to make me worse, and the vomiting was more and more frequent too.

The next morning, I found my mother making breakfast in the kitchen.

"Mom," I said, "do you think you could call Dr. H. and get my medicine changed? I am feeling worse every day. I don't think the lithium is doing a thing to calm me down. Instead, I feel as if I am going faster." "Yes, Maggie, I will call him right now," she responded in a soothing tone.

"I have been worried about that too." As I listened to Mom talk to the doctor, I couldn't help but think she was an angel. She wanted me to get better probably more than I did. "Yes, Doctor, I understand that," I heard her say. "No, I am not giving her any more lithium. Do you understand what I am trying to say? It makes her extremely agitated, thirsty, bloated, and she has severe vomiting." After Mom got off the phone, she said they were going to call this afternoon with the latest blood draw and then they would make a decision based on the results.

Matt came over a little later in the day. I concentrated on trying to stay calm. It was very hard to do and took up every ounce of energy to stay that way.

We were at his house and relaxing by the pool when I said, "Matt, I am so sorry about the way I have treated you these past couple of days. I don't mean to get all crazy on you. The doctors are trying to find a different medicine for me so I can stay in control." "Maggie, that's great," he said. "I am really pulling for you. I really like you a lot, and I want you to get better more than anything." "Matt, do you think we will be together when you go back to school?" "Let's just take it one day at a time," he replied cautiously.

Chapter 39

BIG CHANGES

When I got home, Mom was waiting for me in the living room with the test results.

"Mags, you were right about the medicine," she said. "The doctor said your blood levels were off the charts. It was at a high toxic level, and that is why you have been so sick lately. He said they are starting you on a different form of lithium called Lithobid. We start tomorrow." On Sunday, I went down to the creek to find something to keep me occupied.

I found a bunch of moss floating in the water. I thought it would be fun to make a little statue out of it. Then my mind started slipping again. I started thinking I could contact dead Indians through the statue. I thought if I went down to it at night and had a little ritual, I could talk with the Indians. Many years ago, there was a burial ground in the area. Nobody knew where it was, but it did exist.

After I was satisfied with my creation, I invited my friends Alissa and Cami over. I had not seen them in over a year.

"Hey, girls, great to see you," I said excitedly. "You have to see my moss statue. Come on, let's go down and take a look!" "Maggie, how are you doing?" Allisa asked warily.

"Great! Why wouldn't I be?" I said. "I have had most of the year to do as I please." I actually knew that question was all about my mental situation and why I was in the hospital and other things connected with my condition. We made small talk instead and walked to the creek. I think they were very frightened when I told them that I had the power to contact the dead Indians because they cut our visit short before we could try to contact the Indians.

After they left, I was upset that my friends had taken off so soon. I started yelling at my mother, saying it was her fault they left. My anger got so intense I threatened to kill my mom with a knife. Dad and Tom held me down on the couch while I screamed away. My mania was getting worse and more dangerous. The rest of the evening, I think my parents were in denial, and I had locked myself in the garage.

The next day, I felt like nothing bad had happened and had forgotten all about the incident with Mom. Then Matt walked in.

"Hi, Matt," I said. "Gosh, I sure missed you over the weekend. Nothing to do without you!" "Hey, Mag," he said. "You want to go out or stay here a little while?" he asked.

"Stay here a little bit," I said. "I am kind of wiped out from the weekend." As I lay there on the coach, I suddenly noticed how bad I looked. I hadn't shaved my legs in three days, but I really didn't have the energy anymore to do it.

"Hey, Matt, do you think you could help me with shaving my legs? I am so embarrassed, but I am too exhausted to do it." "No sweat, Mag, I really don't mind," he replied.

So we went upstairs, and he not only shaved my legs, but also washed my hair, which looked pretty greasy and hadn't been washed in weeks. He was too sweet. He knew I was feeling pretty sick to ask him this favor. For the rest of the day, I didn't have my usual energy to drive all over town or go to the lake. The new medication didn't seem to be working yet.

Our week was uneventful due to my feeling so sick. I did enjoy our pool time and a little hockey. My temper tantrums would come on without notice and then leave quickly, and I would forget all about them. My stomach was hurting all the time now. Toward the end of the week, Matt was getting ready to leave for five days for a family Fourth of July get-together at Mammoth Mountain. I was upset that he would be gone so long. I couldn't imagine having to put up with Mom and Dad that entire time. On Thursday night, I didn't want Matt to go home and started to panic.

"Matt, please come back one more time before you leave in the morning," I begged. "I will do the best I can," he said. "Don't worry, I will call and see how you are doing." With that, he pulled away down the driveway; and I was left, feeling increasingly anxious. I couldn't sit still at all. I paced around the garage trying to come up with something to calm me down. Though it was already 10:00 p.m., I decided the best thing to do was go see Matt myself. I waited until midnight before I left.

It was only five miles to his parents' house. I thought that five miles would be nothing for me because I had been a long-distance runner, but I was not thinking about my actual state of health at that moment. First, I cut across a cow pasture to get to a back country road. My mind was really spinning by this time. I thought nothing of what I was doing—whether it was dangerous for me to do it or whether Matt would even want to see me this late. I would run a little, then walk, then run again. When cars passed by, I jumped into the weeds.

After about two miles, I was very tired. Just about that time, I saw two horses by a barn. My mind went into overdrive. Now I could ride to Matt's house! I climbed over the fence and walked softly over the white horse. I put my hand up to him so he would not be afraid of me. Then I reached for his mane and pulled myself up. I had ridden horseback most of my life, so this was easy for me. Plus, there was plenty of moonlight, making it easy to find the way to Matt's house.

I gave the horse a little kick and clicked my tongue at him, and we were off on a trot. I let the horse follow the trail through his own pasture since he was familiar with it. The trail stayed somewhat near the road to Matt's house. Now I could make at least a little ground without walking. I felt free with the wind in my face. Nobody would ever believe I rode a horse in the middle of the night and especially if it was not my horse! After about a mile or so, the trail came to another barn. There was no way I could go any farther. I certainly wasn't going to take the horse out of its pasture. I petted the horse and then hopped over the fence to the road again.

The next two miles seemed endless. My feet hurt; I was tired and thirsty. I began to feel like something was following me. I looked all around me and saw nothing. My head hurt, and I couldn't see straight. I heard a noise on the other side of the fence. I peered over the post to see if there was something there. I thought I saw two gleaming eyes staring back at me. Was I imagining this, or was something lurking in the bushes? I didn't wait to find out and started to run.

I could only go a little way until I was out of breath. I sat down for a while to rest. I figured I could take a shortcut through a pasture and that would land me at about Matt's house. I decided to take the chance, and it worked.

I quietly went down Matt's driveway and tiptoed over to his window.

Trying to avoid making too much noise, I knocked on his window. He didn't stir at first, but when I did it a second time, it startled him. His eyes were wide with shock when he saw me.

"Maggie, what the hell are you doing here?" he said. "It's two in the morning!" "Matt, I just had to see you," I stammered. "I walked, jogged, and even rode a horse to get here. Let me in, will you?" Matt opened the window all the way and helped me through.

"Maggie, I'm beat. I have to get some sleep. Here—you can lie on my bed, and I will take the floor." I was so tired at this point, I didn't argue. I fell asleep within minutes. I felt like I hadn't slept in days. When I awoke, the sun was just starting to peek through, and Matt was nowhere to be seen. I had to get out of his room before his parents caught me. I slipped through the window and started making my way up the driveway. Then I thought I heard Dad calling me. I turned around quickly, and sure enough, there he was. He wasn't mad at me either, which was a huge relief. Matt's parents came out with Matt and said good-bye as Dad put me in his old pickup. Dad told me Mom was taking me on a shopping trip to San Francisco. That got me all excited, and I forgot all about not being able to see Matt.

NOTE: Web sites such as mayoclinic.com and bipolar.com reveal that bipolar patients are at the center of a web composed of caregivers, which often include their family and other loved ones, and various members of the professional community (counselors, therapists, and medical doctors). In the trial-and-error process of prescribing psychotropic medications, doctors sometimes cling to an initial diagnosis out of a misplaced sense of professional pride. Not only can this make the patient's symptoms worse, but it also destroys the doctor's credibility with the patient and her other caregivers. In such situations, some patients and their caregivers make the mistake of trying to do it alone, which is invariably disastrous. However, other patients and their caregivers make the decision to remain within the main parameters of treatment (usually counseling, monitoring, and medication), but may request a reassessment of medication and may make a switch to a different medical professional or team of professionals, part or all of which is often a successful solution to conflicts in treatment of bipolar disorder.

Maggie's Mom – Still Downwardly Diving

(Many of the events that Maggie and I relate are very different around this point in her story. I do not know if things happened the way she remembers - or the way I remember. I only know that if you somehow were able to measure the amount of stress we were under, it would have been off the wall!) Maggie moved into the garage. She hung up posters that she made of the different careers that she would have. The bodyguards came and went. Friends from the third floor came to visit! Joe and I would take turns at night trying to stay awake. Our life was totally out of control, and the only thing we had to hold on to was thinking of that magical moment when the lithium finally worked and our daughter would be ours again.

We went to my niece's wedding in Fresno, which meant an overnight stay in a hotel. Maggie acted up terribly, and Joe had to stay with her and miss the wedding; but there was a small family party afterward we all went to, and Maggie told everyone there how mean her parents were. She swore at us and at everyone in general. We don't use swearwords—so we were shocked at her language. I finally couldn't take it anymore and told her to clean up her mouth when she talked to me or else. (What on earth the "or else" would have been, I do not know—but she did quit. She didn't call my bluff, and I remember feeling some little success, however modest it was.) On another day, she showed up at the high school when Tom was practicing for his senior track season. He would not tell me what she did, but he asked me to keep her from coming around his friends. Not long after, we got a call from a woman who said she thought *Maggie* was in trouble in the town of *Sonora*. *Joe* went to get her. *He* found her, but she ran away. *My* husband is not fast, but he is dogged, and he told me later that he just followed her no matter where she ran until he caught up with her on *Stockton Street*—one of the main thoroughfares.

As he grabbed her, a car went by and *Maggie* started shouting that this man was attacking her. *Fortunately*, the ladies in the car knew *Joe* and *Maggie* and drove on.

Once when we drove into a *McDonald's*, *Maggie* said that if we didn't do what she wanted, she would tell the lady at the drive-through window that her dad was molesting her! *I* was so shocked, *I* threw a whole cup of ice water in her face. She was so shocked that she sat back and shut up! *Donna Reese*, who had commiserated with me at *Christmastime*, (how long ago that seemed!) called to say her son, *Matt*, was home from college and was available for the bodyguard job. *I* said *I'd* let her know and put his name on the list. About a week later, his name had moved up to the top, and *Matt* was the next in line. *He* was older, responsible, seemed to genuinely care for *Maggie*, and wonder of wonders, she listened to him. *When* he said she needed to calm down, it was as if a switch turned off! (*I* remember thinking that at last the medicine is starting to work.) *He* took her up to a beautiful mountain park called *Pinecrest*, to the movies, to the downtown scene—in fact, he took her everywhere she wanted to go and seemed to be able to handle it all (at least he didn't quit in three days).

One day, *I* asked *Matt* to take *Maggie* down to *Modesto* to her psychiatric appointment. *When* they got back, *Maggie* ran into the house telling me that her doctor had gone on vacation and that she had seen another doctor and that he told her he felt she was just fine and didn't need any medication at all! She said he had taken her off the lithium completely! *I* called the doctor's office to find out if that was true. *No* one would talk to me (of course) until *I* threatened to come down and do a sit-down strike in the office, then I explained that I just wanted to know if what she told me was accurate. After about thirty minutes, the new psychiatrist she had spoken with did call me. He indicated that, yes, her regular doctor was on vacation; and yes, he had seen Maggie; and yes, he, the doctor she had seen that day, felt that the lithium was not working. She was up to 2,500 milligrams a day, and he said that we should see what happened if she stopped taking so much. Then he said, "I was so impressed with your daughter—I think she is just fine!" I could not believe my ears. I questioned Maggie pretty hard; she had a sly look on her face, and I wondered if she had a newfound power that included telling people whatever she felt they wanted to hear.

That night, she slept upstairs in her room. Joe didn't like the looks of things and slept outside of her door on the floor because he was so worried. About two in the morning, he came down and told me she was gone. We ran outside to check her bedroom window; it turned out that she had tied sheets together for a rope and used it to climb out of her window.

Joe got the car and drove around the county. I got a flashlight and walked all over our property, calling and crying out for her. At dawn, we both came home to wait for the phone call, any phone call. It finally came—from Matt's mother.

Maggie had walked to his house. Joe went to get her, and while he was gone, I finally realized I had had it! I had taken as much, and more, than I could; and it was time to do something! I called the emergency number for the Modesto psychiatrist. They finally put me through to the new psychiatrist. I told him what had happened—and I let him have it for a while! When I finally calmed down and ran out of breath, I told him he owed me the answer to one question. He agreed he did; and I asked that if Maggie were his daughter, what he would do. He was silent for a minute and then said he would try to get her into the psychiatric unit at Stanford

Medical Center in Palo Alto. I asked how to do that, and he said that first I had to find out if they had a bed available. I slammed down the phone and sobbed for a while. Then I picked it back up, figured out how to call Stanford, finally reached the right department, and was told they had a bed available but we would have to have the doctor admit her. I called the psychiatrist back, got him to call Stanford and admit her, and was ready to go by the time Joe got back from picking Maggie up.

Maggie was flushed with her success of her great escape. Joe had gotten one of the men who worked for us to ride with us to Stanford in case she gave us trouble. His name, by coincidence, was also Matt. He sat in the back seat with her for the three-hour trip. Joe had told him to be ready to hold her down if she lunged for the wheel or the door and to be ready for anything. When I look back on this, I think this was the single most foolish thing we did; we should have gotten an ambulance to take her.

Even so, we made the trip successfully. (Later, she said when I told her we were taking her to Stanford, she thought we would be going shopping at the big shopping mall! I would have told any lie to get her in that car that day.) They weren't ready for her, so Matt got a wheelchair, put her in it, and treated her like the Queen of May just going for a ride. It worked; he kept her busy for the hour or so we had to wait. She was finally called for an "intake" examination. A little while later, the staff told us to go home and that they would admit her immediately. We didn't even say good-bye. We just got in the car, drove home, and slept for twenty-four hours

Chapter 40

STANFORD

When Dad and I got home, Mom had already packed a bag for me. Dad said he was going too. I thought that a little odd since we were going shopping. On our way, we stopped by the feed store. Dad said one of his workers needed a ride over to the Bay Area. Now I really thought that was out of the ordinary, but what could I say? I was getting to go shopping. As we got closer to the city, I noticed we were exiting the freeway in the wrong direction.

"Dad, where are we going?" I questioned. "Don't worry, Mags, we just need to stop off at Stanford for a minute," Mom replied. This was really confusing me. Why did we need to go to Stanford? I had been there many times for running, but that was it. It didn't take us long before we pulled up in front of a huge brick building that looked like a hospital.

"Maggie, we are just checking a doctor out real quick before we go shopping," Mom calmly stated. "All right, I guess that's fine," I said. I looked over my shoulder and noticed Dad's worker (by coincidence, his name is Matt) was coming in too. Maybe he was coming in because he didn't want to sit in the car.

As I went into the hospital, little did I know I wouldn't be coming out until twenty-two long days later. I began to get a little nervous as Mom went up to the check-in window. Dad could sense this and had Matt take me for a walk through the hospital lobby.

"Hey, Maggie, don't worry," Matt offered. "Well, how can I not be worried, Mom and Dad said I was going shopping," I anxiously replied.

"I bet you will get to go—just not right this minute," he countered. "Hey, Maggie, how about a little fun. I will wheel you around in the wheelchair! Come on." I agreed, and we toured around as if I was handicapped. It did keep my anxiety at bay. The hospital was really big with many lobby areas. We stopped at one room where a harpist was playing beautiful music to a group of patients.

I was transfixed by the beautiful sounds. After the song ended, the harpist came over and handed me a CD. I was surprised and delighted to get a free CD! On our way back, Matt chatted with me about his work and what he was up to. He was very nice, and the calmness of his voice kept me from worrying about why we were really here.

When we got back, my parents said the doctor was ready to see me. I thought that very odd but went along with it. Matt said he would walk me into the room, which I greatly appreciated. I felt very nervous about this situation.

Was this some kind of trick? Was this place another mental institution? Matt and I went into a small room that had only one chair and some kind of security camera in the corner.

"Hey, Maggie," Matt said. "Don't hold back, all right? Just let them see how you really are, then you can get better sooner." Before I had a chance to reply, he left me in the small room. I began to panic, being alone. I tried the door, but it was locked. Then I really freaked out and started yelling at the door, but nobody came. In an instant, I knew that I had been tricked. There would be no shopping trip, and I would not be leaving this place today. I went over and sat on the chair and tried to remain calm. Maybe if I could convince the doctor I was perfectly fine, they would let me go home—but that didn't work at all because my mind started to race, and I could not control my anger. I could feel it starting to push up my throat until I started screaming at the camera mounted on the wall.

"Let me out now!" I wailed. "If you don't let me out of here, I will bust that door down. I know you crackpots are watching me! I am not stupid, you jerks! You want to see if I am crazy. Here is crazy, you idiots!" Then I made a nasty, insulting gesture to the camera.

I knew this wasn't going to help my case, but I could not control my rage.

I picked up the chair and threw it against the door. That got their attention.

An orderly came in and took the chair and closed the door before I could do anything. I kept on screaming until my throat became sore, and then I started throwing myself against the door. Three orderlies came in, grabbed me, and strapped me down to a gurney. As they took me down the hall, my parents watched in horror. I vividly remember seeing Mom as we went by; she was sobbing as my father turned her away from the awful scene.

Journal Entry - July 4, 1996

Everything is bad, horrible . . . I am gone in my head . . . They got me . . . I am in a mental institution at Stanford. On the best holiday ever. No family fun . . . No nothing . . . Crazy people, rules, white walls, nurses, restrictions, bad people. I saw the fireworks on TV. I am really, really angry!

Chapter 41

ESCAPE

I didn't write in my journal for the twenty-two days I was there. I was too sick to do so.. I don't remember every detail of my stay at Stanford, as I did at Tuolumne General, but still can recall quite a lot for being so ill. Within the first hour, I was scheming ways of trying to escape. Dad had warned the nurses that I was extremely clever and that they had to really watch me. They assured Dad that Stanford has a double-lockdown security system so that nobody could escape.

One day I do remember that I saw, every hour or so, the nurses changed shifts. Since I had not yet changed into hospital clothing, I went up to the nurses' station and tapped on the glass, right after the shift change. The nurse came out and asked me what I needed. She was just beginning her shift and had no idea that I had just been admitted.

I thought it was worth a try, so I said, "I am all done visiting my sister. Can I be buzzed through please." The nurse replied, "Certainly, have a nice day!" That was it! I was a free bird! Immediately, I was on the other side, and my head was spinning out of control. I could no longer control myself to stay calm.

The first thing I remember thinking was that I was in the movie Terminator. I thought I was Sarah Connor and was being hunted by a killer robot. I ran through the hallways, looking for an escape route. Suddenly, sirens began wailing, and red lights flashed in every hall! Then white-coated staff members converged on me from all directions and tackled me to the ground.

All I remember is shrieking in pain and biting at the white coats. One of them yelled, "She bit me!" They dragged me kicking and screaming back to the so-called secure unit. I made such a commotion in the unit that all the patients had to be locked in their rooms. They laid me flat on my back and strapped me down, including my hands, head, chest, legs, and feet. I could only move my eyes! I was screaming nonstop until I felt the sting of a hypodermic needle full of sedative.

Being in four-point restraints on the Fourth of July was an experience I shall never forget. Now, I truly appreciate freedom.

Chapter 42

PRIVILEGES

As I mentioned, at Stanford I did not keep a journal—partly because there was no time to do so. The doctors and nurses kept me very busy with arts and crafts, classes on how to manage my illness, medications, sleeping, eating, and group sessions. Also, my mind was so far gone that writing would have been impossible. In fact, my doctors on the ward classified me as a Code I and a Code III in my charts. Code I meant that I was a danger to myself, and Code III meant that I was severely disabled.

I had next to no privileges. There are four levels of the H2 Stanford Health Services Guidelines: Level 1 Patient is restricted to the unit Level 2A Patient may leave unit only if escorted by 1:1 staff Level 2B Patient may leave the unit as part of a group escorted by staff Level 3 Patient may leave the unit unaccompanied by staff. Patients may go to the patio only. Patients must check in with nursing staff every thirty minutes. Patio privileges may be used between the hours of 7:15 a.m. and 9:00 p.m. Supervised fifteen-minute patio breaks occur daily at 8:30 a.m., 10:45 a.m., 2:00 p.m., 4:30 p.m., 6:30 p.m., and 8:30 p.m.

My privileges were few for the most part as I was at level 1 for quite a long time. I don't remember when I finally graduated to level 2A and 2B. I was in Stanford University's psychiatric ward for a little over three weeks. Fortunately for us, we had no "Nurse Ratcheds." Though the staff had many rules, and my privileges were few, I remember an intelligent, caring staff that wanted to get all of us rehabilitated and back into the real world.

Chapter 43

REMEMBERING

I can only remember my twenty-two days locked up in Stanford Medical Center's psychiatric ward in bits and pieces. I remember some of the other patients there, like Otto. He was an older Jewish man who told me of his days as a child in a German concentration camp. When I complained about how bad we were being treated, and how awful it was being confined, he showed me his tattooed wrists and let me know, beyond any doubt, that things could always be worse.

I met another bipolar patient there too. His name was Rich, and he was also manic. Another woman, Darla, was bipolar and was going through electroshock treatments so that she could get off her medication to have a child.

My roommate was Martha, a beautiful young girl with obsessive-compulsive disorder. She had perfectly straight long red hair. She would brush her hair constantly to the point that it would fall out. Martha was obsessed with keeping everything in strict order, and it seems strange that they would room her with a bipolar patient going through a chaotic, manic episode. I also became acquainted with other patients, but I was so sick at the time I can't remember them specifically.

One part of Stanford that I remember very clearly was going to a beautiful garden on breaks. I would pretend it was a magical place and would bring my mind back. It had a huge stone wall that was covered with sweeping colorful vines, pretty flowers, and a nice green lawn. I remember running around in circles to let my energy unwind. The other patients were always amazed by the stories I told on break. I told them how successful a runner I was and that I would be in the Olympics soon. I also told them about my acting career and how I had been in several movies and would be in more as soon as I got well. The other patients seemed to believe my stories and would ask me lots of questions about my "amazing" life. Of course, this was all part of my mania and delusions of grandeur, but I was so completely deluded that I not only convinced myself, but others as well.

During my stay, I found out that one of our good family friends, Suzie Vasko, was also a patient at Stanford. She was thirty-two and had Hodgkin's lymphoma. She was on another floor undergoing chemotherapy, and her family stayed with her. I briefly remember seeing Suzie and her mom, Barbara, but that's all I can recall. Mom told me later that she and Barbara cried quite a bit together over their young, sick children. Suzie eventually made a full recovery.

Maggie's Mom - Stanford

Again, I can only relate in no particular order the things that happened.

The cost was unbelievable: approximately $7,000 a day! We had to give them a check for $10,000 the day she was admitted and then were scheduled at the business office soon after so they could determine how we intended to pay.

They told us that our private insurance company had a poor record of paying for mental claims and we should not count on them. Joe said that was odd since they had paid the 80 percent from her first hospitalization with no problem. The business officer then asked if I would find out exactly how the business office had managed to get them to pay.

After I got home from Palo Alto, I talked with Lisa, the clerk in the Tuolumne General business office. She gave me the exact verbiage she used on the forms, and I relayed it to the Stanford business office. Wonder of wonders, the insurance company started paying their 80 percent immediately, and I am sure that Stanford made good use of their new verbiage (I like to think that this was one of those mysterious ways that God worked. I wonder how many people were probably helped by the hiring of a young girl to watch my children when Joe and I went out on a date night so long ago.

This Lisa was a young girl who liked my kids and was grateful for the money we paid her and who remembered me and was willing to help when Maggie was in serious need.) Maggie was at Stanford for twenty-two days. If you do the math, you can see that our 20 percent of the payment for her stay was still daunting. Friends at home wanted to have a benefit for us (a spaghetti dinner as I remember).

Joe and I resisted that—it just wasn't how we do things, and the thought of not taking care of our own children was anathema to us. So we took out a second mortgage on our house. And yet when Joe's dad sent us a check, followed shortly by my mother sending one too, it was such a feeling of relief to know that our families were behind us and would do what they could. Even my uncle John wrote to say he would be glad to help us with Maggie's bills. We thanked him but said no, we could handle it—but how lovely it was that he offered! I spent most of my days sitting outside the Stanford psych ward double-door system, waiting to see Maggie. When I did get in, I saw the same kind of behavior from Maggie that I had seen on the third floor of Toulumne General. She was rude, she yelled at everyone, she was obnoxious; but what was remarkably different was the reaction of the staff. They treated her as if she just didn't know what she was doing. They were always courteous and quiet; they never raised their voices and were firm and deliberate in their statements and actions.

I learned a lot from them. They treated Maggie like what she was—a sick girl— not an awful, screaming harridan. They were real professional caregivers.

The doctors at Stanford changed her medication immediately. They told us that the lithium was obviously not working, and they were changing her to the new drug of choice for Maggie's kind of illness, Depakote. Still, it would be at least fourteen days before they would be able to tell if it was working.

Meanwhile, Maggie started working the system to get out almost from the second day she was there. She had been admitted on a fourteen-day hold, so she couldn't get anywhere with her screams and demands. (Which led me to think that she would forget about it—ha! Not so!) I got a phone call from my friend Donna one day. She told me that Maggie was calling collect from Stanford for Matt. I wasn't sure if she was upset because Maggie was calling or upset because it was collect. When I asked at the hospital, they told me that when Maggie cooperated with the staff, she could earn points—and she spent her points on those collect calls. I wished that just one of those calls would come for me, but I never got one.

One day, I was down in the Stanford cafeteria, and alarms went off all over the hospital. Something told me it was Maggie, and I ran back up to the psych ward. They would not let me in and would not tell me if anything was wrong, but as I sat there in the hall, six huge men in white shirts and black pants (I remember what they wore and how their faces looked—red and flushed and angry) were pushing a gurney, and on the gurney was my beautiful daughter.

She was strapped down, and something was in her mouth so she could not yell, and her blue eyes were staring intently at me as she went past. They took her back into the unit, and I didn't get to see her for two days.

I remember the lowest point in my life. Barbara, a friend who knew I was there and whose daughter Suzie was coming to Stanford for chemo treatments, pried me away from my seat in the hall one day. We went down to the cancer center for Suzie's treatment. Suzie was—and is—a free spirit who has a zest for life! Over her bald head, she was wearing a knit hat with two long tresses of her hair pinned to the sides! She was a favorite with the nurses; she got lots of love and hugs and "how are you doing, sweetie?" greetings.

After they set her up for the treatment, one of the nurses came into our curtained cubicle and told us that a new patient was just coming in for her first treatment. She asked Suzie if she would mind talking to her. Of course not— back went the curtain, and in the next bed was a beautiful girl with long dark hair and big scared eyes. I remember the parents; they seemed gray to me. I even think they were dressed in gray, and their eyes were the same as hers— just big and scared. Suzie prattled happily on, answering questions about hair and food and I don't know what all—and all of a sudden, I felt that my cheeks were wet. I know I didn't make a sound, but my blouse was getting wet. Barbara realized I was breaking down and took me out of the room.

I kept saying, "I don't know why I'm crying," and she looked at me, paused, and said, "Yes, you do." And, of course, I did: there I was, wishing my daughter had cancer! I am crying again as I write this—I actually wished for that awful, awful disease just because it was a definable thing! At fourteen days, we found that Maggie had not forgotten that her hold was up. She announced that she was checking herself out and that there was nothing we could do about it. Joe and I met with the doctors and the head of the ward.

They told us that they felt the Depakote was beginning to work and that one more week would likely do it. They told us they were going to call Maggie's bluff—that they would agree to let her see a judge, but would be sure to explain to her what that would entail. The judge for that county was headquartered in San Jose. Maggie would be taken down in handcuffs to testify, and the doctor and head of the unit would be there to testify as to why the judge should not grant her freedom.

However, they also warned us that if she still wanted to leave, and if the judgment was against us, we would have to agree that we would let her walk out onto the streets of a big city and disappear! Joe and I looked at each other in horror. The doctors said that if we *were not prepared to do whatever the judge decided, they didn't want to make the effort and waste a whole day. I remember thinking at least they wanted to help us this time—and we agreed. When we returned to the hall, Joe turned to me and said that, no matter what, we wouldn't let her just walk away from us. I collapsed in his arms and wept in relief.*

Maggie was thrilled with the idea of the ride in the police car and practiced what she would say to the judge; but when the moment came, and they approached her with the handcuffs, she gave in and signed the "seven-day hold" papers. I still shudder to think of the slender thread that had supported our hopes of keeping Maggie safe and in treatment.

At about sixteen days, they let me take Maggie into the garden by herself.

She was quiet, she was interested in the plants, she told me she felt better. By day 19, there was a remarkable change. I felt hopeful for the first time in a long time; they let us take Maggie out with us for a day. We took her best friend, Carrie, with us, and we all went to the beach. As I saw the two of them walking together once again, down by the sand, the hope in my heart took a leap; and I thought, "Maybe, just maybe, we are on the right road at last."

On day 22, she was discharged, and we went home. My job was just beginning, but she was clearly our Maggie again. She slept all the way.

Amy's View - Stanford

During the time Maggie was hospitalized at Stanford, my mom stayed with me at the apartment in San Francisco I shared with four other flight attendants.

We kind of had an agreement—no guests—but my friends realized this was different and bent the rules for us. My mom did all sorts of chores and cooked for whoever was home and left for the hospital every day. The first time I was able to go was hard for me. This was not my sister—this was a scared, confused, unreal person. But in two weeks, things looked better: the new medication was starting to work—Maggie started slowing down; she looked genuinely glad to see me. One more week and home they went—for a long time of recovery and learning; but at least, our family was all marching forward in tandem again.

Chapter 44

HALFWAY

After twenty-two days in Stanford's psychiatric ward, I was relocated to a halfway house that would help me cope with the world at large. It was a beautiful house full of people who were hoping to recover after their time in the mental ward. Everyone was over thirty-five, so right away I did not like it. Mom and Dad said I had to try it though. That evening, as I lay in a strange bed, I thought about Matt. I couldn't see him for the duration of my stay, so if it was going to be a couple of months, I had to devise a plan. I decided I would talk my parents into living with them at home and doing an outpatient program at Stanford twice a week. At that time, I felt that my main purpose for following the rules and taking all the medication I was prescribed was to get back to Matt. I would do anything to be with him! My parents agreed to the plan as long as I followed it. So I got to go home.

I did come through with everything as promised, and Mom and I traveled over to Palo Alto twice a week for my group session and to meet with my doctor. It was not easy, but I did attend the meetings. As strange as it sounds, I actually grieved a little over losing my manic side. All that creativity and incredible energy were gone. After a four-month extreme high, I was coming back to reality. It was like Alice leaving wonderland—I felt like I was losing a part of myself or like I was losing a friend. My family was very supportive through my recovery. Mom faithfully drove me to my appointments and listened to my rants, Dad kept his business together and gave me a shoulder to cry on, my sister came home regularly to visit me, and my brother was pulling for me too.

Our family had weathered a major storm, but full recovery was still a long way away.

NOTE: Recovery in and of itself is an ongoing process. Once the patient's moods have stabilized, and she is again able to function in the world at large and enjoy life, the process of maintaining this desirable state is a combination of continued medication (and at times adjusting medication), self-monitoring combined with counseling, periodic medical checkups, and sometimes ongoing group sessions. The tools used in all this have to do with communication. The person with bipolar disorder keeps a daily mood chart to stay alert of unusual ups or downs, writes a daily journal (which is usually shared with a psychological counselor), stays in touch with caregivers and others who are intimately associated with the well-being of the bipolar person, and may attend group sessions to share information with others recovering from bipolar disorder. A strong spiritual life is also essential—the precepts of twelve-step programs read as if they are based (and they are!) on basic Christian principles. God gives spiritual strength to all who seek His help. A daily prayer life helps one to stay on the track of love and humility and care for others even as we care for ourselves. This helps those who are recovering from bipolar disorder to defeat the delusional hubris that comes with manic attacks as well as the horrific despair associated with deep depression. If this sounds like a lot to do, it is well worth it. As has been said, "The price of freedom is eternal vigilance." That political slogan definitely applies to the core of every human being. Rather than being enslaved by tyrannical mental states, those recovering from bipolar disorder invest a little extra time to maintain awareness and to keep the channels of communication open with those who can help them— including both the human sphere and the divine. (Information gleaned from Girl Interrupted, mayoclinic.com, and bipolar.com.)

Chapter 45

RECOVERY

The first thing I did when I got home from Stanford was to call Matt immediately.

I wanted so badly to see him. He showed up with flowers, a hug, and a smile I'll never forget. Our friendship blossomed into a wonderful romance in the weeks that followed. I was so enthralled with the way he made me feel normal. He was positive, supportive, and he made me want to get well. We ended up dating for the next six years and finally married in San Diego in March of 2002. He is the love of my life and is truly my bodyguard! My family went on to help me through the months of recovery ahead. It was still tough for me, especially as I come to realize that I had lost many friends and how mean I had been to everybody—especially my family—and the horrible things I said to my best friend, Carrie, and all the harassment I had given to Matt. Some days I just would want the manic side back so I wouldn't have to think about trying so hard to be well. But I knew if I did not take my medicine, I would destroy myself, my family, and everything we had all worked so hard for. Over the next four months, with the help of doctors, counselors, and a loving family, I finally began to feel like my old self.

By January 1997, I moved to downtown San Francisco, got a job, went to school, and lived on my own. My family was so supportive with the move that it helped me become a confident young woman again. Without their help, I know I would have ended up dead. Words cannot describe how thankful I am to have such a loving family who helped me through times that were extremely hard for all of us, and a best friend who didn't give up on me, and my bodyguard Matt who did not desert me no matter what and always believed in me.

I had been through hell for nine months, which seemed like nine years, but finally, once again I was Maggie Hurst.

Matt and I got married March 23, 2002. (Courtesy Rich Miller Photography)

Maggie's Mania from Donna Reese's Perspective

Beautiful, fun-loving Maggie crashed into our lives the summer her family hired my son Matt as her bodyguard. I thought this a strange job, but it did seem to suit my son's easygoing nature and dislike for strenuous labor. What college guy wouldn't love to drive this cute babe to all the hot spots in town and hang out with her? If Matt could have written his own job description for that summer home from college, I doubt that he could have dreamed up anything more appealing.

The first week, I gave the motherly lecture on this being a professional job and that Matt shouldn't become emotionally invested in this girl. Maggie zoomed in and out of our home that week as they came by to use the pool or attend a youth gathering. As hard as Maggie tried, she didn't fit in with her former classmates that she was becoming reacquainted with at various summer functions. She would blurt out things that didn't always connect with the topic of conversation, and she would become giddy over the smallest hint of humor in any situation. Maggie was either ballistic or bombastic or silly or insulting, but seldom was she appropriate-teenager or not.

I begin to see this wasn't the easy job I had envisioned for Matt. He came home increasingly later each evening and thoroughly exhausted. He seemed strung out as the job eventually demanded all of his attention. At the time, we had no idea that Maggie's mania was increasing or that Matt became the one stable thing in her life that she clung to. As long as she was with him, she believed she could hang on and not go over the edge. There was more truth to this part of her thinking than we realized.

I began to mentor Maggie spiritually, hoping that I could help her get through this apparent rough spot in her life. I prayed with her and shared simple scriptures of encouragement. Although she was open to God being a part of her life, she showed an inability to concentrate, and her eyes darted in multiple directions as I tried to establish eye contact. Her hands shook, and sometimes she vomited, and now and then, her eyes would roll back in her head as her body was trying to assimilate the drugs the doctors had prescribed for her.

Poor Maggie, I thought, as I prayed the doctors would come to understand her condition and give her the proper treatment. She definitely was not well or safe to leave alone. I came to understand the need for a bodyguard. Her parents couldn't watch her all day and were desperately trying to give her some semblance of a normal, carefree summer. It became obvious she did not have the proper judgment to care for herself, let alone drive.

Maggie's mania climaxed when she "needed" Matt and simply jogged to our home in the middle of a dark country night. She arrived at Matt's bedroom window, thinking that made perfect sense. In the early morning, when I learned of Maggie's surprise appearance, she was still sleeping when we contacted her parents. Her dad, Joe, arrived for an early breakfast as we waited for Maggie to wake up. We talked, and I saw a father's deep love and care and desire to get his daughter the best medical help available. As we sat in our bay window breakfast nook, we saw Maggie slipping by right in front of us, thinking she was invisible to us. I realized the seriousness of this precious girl's mental illness. My heart simply ached for Maggie and her wonderful family, and I wanted to wave a magic wand over her and transform her into a princess awakening from a nightmare.

We called a ranch hand to help contain Maggie if needed, and when they took Maggie away, it was a terrible scene that will stay in my memory forever: Joe and the ranch hand bodily picked up Maggie, all the while she was kicking and screaming and fearful and shouting, "no, no, no, I don't want to go!" Her sanity had slipped away just as she was being taken from her "savior," Matt.

I felt empty, drained, helpless, and upset as I tried to process that horrible scene in my mind. Off to the Stanford Medical Center psychiatric ward. Surely they could help her, or was she beyond help? It was very painful seeing her hauled off against her will, yet I knew this was better being out of our hands.

The love of her family was leading them to do the right thing. Little did I realize that day, that the seeds of love between my son and Maggie had already been planted in this strange beginning relationship, which would ultimately and triumphantly endure and withstand the test of love. Maggie became the daughter-in-law whom I dearly love and adore today.

I am now so proud of the way Maggie valiantly fought her illness and compliantly followed her doctor's directions. I am also proud of Matt to let his love for this woman be more powerful than her mental illness and to pledge to love and care for her "until death do them part." Thank you, God, for answering our prayers of healing for Maggie in a way I could never have envisioned. Praise the Lord!

Maggie's Mom - An In-between Time

Now we entered a new time. Maggie and I drove back to Stanford three days a week so that she could be in the outpatient program. We would leave early at four in the morning, driving to the Bay Area. I would wake Maggie up when we went across the bridge so I could count as a car pool. (Now I realize how ridiculous that was; the outpatient program cost $600 a day, and I was trying to save two bucks!) She would check in by 8:00 a.m. and stay all day.

I usually spent my day either in the Stanford Medical Library trying to learn anything new about being bipolar or wandering around the big shopping mall.

I would pick up Maggie; we would go to dinner and then to a little inexpensive hotel for the night. The next day would be the same, and then at 5:00 p.m. on the third day, we would drive the three hours home.

This was our schedule for the next three weeks. I think it was probably the most important time for Maggie because she began to finally understand that just because she was ill, her life was not over. It was during this time that Stanford assigned a new psychiatrist to us. Dr. Garfield was a wonderful, intelligent woman who took a real interest in Maggie. We went once a week during our three-day visits. She saw Maggie for a whole hour each time and also talked to me frankly about the things Maggie was going through. I was always grateful that she did that. I never felt that she shut me out because she was worried about patient-privilege problems.

During one of those three-day ordeals, I went to downtown Palo Alto to have lunch. As I was sitting in one of the outdoor cafés, I saw a bag lady on the sidewalk, pushing a shopping cart that was full of her stuff. I was shocked to realize that I knew her. Her name was Carol, and she had been one of Maggie's fellow patients at the Stanford psychiatric ward. I asked her to park her cart next to my table, and I bought her lunch, to the dismay of the restaurant staff. (The manager came to ask if I was being bothered; when I told him I had invited her, he went away—but not happily.) I remembered that Carol was about forty-five, but she looked seventy. She had very few teeth. She told me that she was bipolar and "just had a hard time keeping it together." About once a month, she would try to cause enough trouble to get the police to pick her up. They would lock her up for a seventy-two-hour hold, during which she would bathe, eat good food, get good meds, and then out they sent her again. I asked her how long she had been in the area; she told me three years and that it was the best time in her life. I gave her all the money I had—probably twenty dollars—and then watched her cart on down the sidewalk, praying that it wasn't Maggie's future I was watching.

I saw Carol over the next few months—sometimes just on the street, most times with her cart full of stuff. She was always glad to see me and always told me she was getting along okay. I always gave her what money I had on me. Then I didn't see her anymore. I don't know what happened to her.

Meanwhile, Maggie's visits to Stanford went down to two per week, then one per week, and then one every other week. When we went to Stanford, Maggie usually slept in the morning, but was very talkative coming home, full of information and coping strategies. Otherwise, she would call Matt (he was back at college). Still, she was lonely; all her friends were going on with their lives, and the ones who were left in town were afraid of her. It was a tough time, but it was also a time in which I finally saw her inner strength starting to shine through. It was a "well, that's the way it is, and I need to deal with it" attitude that I had never seen in Maggie before.

Maggie caught me up straight one day. I am sure I was going on and on about bipolar disorder and how it wasn't the end of the world, as usual, when she looked at me and said, "Mom, it's my disease you know!" I will never forget that moment, because she was right; I was trying to share a burden that could not be shared.

At one point, I decided to try to do something that might really help my daughter. I had begun to realize how stigmatized she was by the term "mentally ill," and how unfair it all was. So I put together a box of all the information I had gathered up at Stanford, plus a brief story of her life, as a store of information to loan to people who might be interested in really knowing about bipolar disorder. This would thereafter be known as the Maggie Box.

I also resolved to talk openly about mental illness (when the opportunity arose) and its role in our lives. Wonder of wonders, when people asked about my three children and what they were doing, I would report on Amy's wonderful career as a flight attendant who flies all over the world, and Thomas who majored in business at the maritime academy, and I would then say as frankly as I could that Maggie was struggling with a difficult disorder, that she was bipolar, and we were all feeling our way through it. I swear that of every ten people I told, seven would say they had some experience with mental illness in their family and that they usually didn't talk about it. Then we would hang on each other's neck for a moment and then talk. If they were desperate, I offered the Maggie Box.

The rules are simple: keep it as long as necessary, add any thing you think might help someone else, make copies of anything you would like, and send it back for the next person who might need it.

The Maggie Box has crisscrossed the United States many times; it has even been to Italy to a woman I met in a painting class.

Usually, it can be gone for a month or so, come back in the mail, be put back on the shelf, and within just a few days, another opportunity for it to be shared just comes sailing along. Again, I think of those mysterious ways.

Maggie started to talk about what she would do with her life. She talked about fashion school (she loved shopping) and thought that might be a good fit for her. I myself liked the idea of a school that was directly oriented toward a career and not full of stressful classes like algebra! We began to investigate.

About this time, Maggie's doctor called me into her office at the end of a session at Stanford. She told me that she and Maggie had agreed that Maggie was ready to be in charge of her own medication—and thanked me for keeping Maggie alive and well. She then relieved me of that obligation. Wasn't that an amazing way of telling me to butt out? I got the message. But the next morning, when I heard Maggie get up and go down the hall to the bathroom, and I found myself desperately trying to hear if she was unscrewing the cap to her meds, I knew I was in trouble! I had taken over her life; I was a fraud.

I could talk the talk about how independent and strong Maggie was becoming, but I could not walk the walk! I looked at the local paper that I was clenching in my hands and inwardly wailed, How on earth can I not ask her if she took her meds? Then another one of those mysterious things happened. A classified ad in the paper was catching my attention, "looking out of the paper" right at me. It said, "Artist Studio $100 a month" and gave a phone number. I called, told the lady I would be right up, grabbed my purse, yelled up to Maggie that I was going out for a couple of hours, and literally ran out of the house.

The "Artist Studio" was little more than a cold garage. I rented it anyway and went to the local art store and bought some paper and pencils and a little table and chair and sat there—with the garage door up so I could get some light—and drew for an hour. I had graduated from college with my BA in fine arts, but it had been thirty years since I had drawn a thing! But it worked. Every time I felt myself opening my mouth to ask if Maggie had taken her medicine, I would clench my jaw and run for the car. I began to let go of the worry for ten, sometimes twenty, minutes at a time. I tried to stay in my studio all morning—and sometimes stretched it into the afternoon. My talent had "gone a glimmering," but very occasionally, I'd see something I liked about what I had drawn—and I liked enough that I finally ordered some paints.

Maggie found a fashion school in San Francisco that she wanted to attend.

I took her over for the entrance exam, and she passed with flying colors. We found a safe place for her to live: the San Francisco Women's Club, just across the street from the Fairmont Hotel. She had a furnished room, and the monthly fee included meals, and there seemed to be lots of young people staying there, from around the world who were studying in San Francisco. She started the spring term and liked the school, and the job that came with it—working at the Limited downtown, selling hot, cute clothes! She was off and running with new purpose and a new direction.

Now I went to my garage in earnest! Painting helped my mind focus on something else than just worrying, and I began to live again too.

Allie and Maggie visit Amy on the job. (Courtesy the Hurst family)

Amy's View - Finding How I Fit in Maggie's Life

Over the years, I had to learn what my role in Maggie's life was. My natural inclination was to be the "big-sister fixer"—in fact, I remember I found a really cool keychain with a watertight container that could hold two or three of her pills—so just in case she forgot or lost those precious meds that kept her alive, she would always have one with her. I have no idea whether or not she ever used it, but it made me feel better! I know there were times when I would let my parents know that she was a little over the top or seemed a little down.

Sometimes they would come for a few days, sometimes I would just arrange a visit. Sometimes I would just do six or seven loads of laundry, and that would do it; other times I would take her to lunch or the movies. I learned that sometimes a big sister can just be there—for the big things or the small things— just be there.

Maggie's Mom – The Following Years

Maggie did well at fashion school, though she seemed to get a little "fast" later in the spring. She went to her psychiatrist in Palo Alto by herself every other week. They may have tweaked her medication a bit; I was out of the loop! Summer came, and she came home for three months. It was brutally hot, and the heat seemed to really affect her. She saw Matt during the summer— they went on real dates she said. She also made arrangements to move to the Los Angeles campus of the fashion school. We found a cute apartment that was deemed a safe place to live. She would be close to her grandparents and a caring aunt, so we felt it was a good move. And of course, we realized it was closer to Matt, who was finishing up at the university in Riverside. After a second semester, Maggie decided that fashion was not her game. She told us it was a cutthroat business, and when the stress started to increase, she didn't feel very good. Her doctor agreed, and so we looked for a new direction.

She enrolled at Pasadena City College for the next semester. She did well until the late spring and then had trouble again. A pattern was emerging.

Winters were dark and sad; summers hot and excited. Even she was beginning to accept what was happening. If she had As in her classes until at least May, she would be able to finish with a C by the end of the term. We just lumbered along.

Now looking back, I can see that this seemingly aimless "looking for something" time was very important. A bipolar patient is unsure of who they are, and they have no clue about what they can do, so the only thing to do is just try new things until something sticks! Matt was moving to San Diego, so Maggie decided that was a good place for her too. Actually, by then, I had learned a lot about how her surroundings affected her, so we agreed, providing that she live out by the beach. At the beach, the temperature does not change much from winter to summer. She had such a terrible time handling inland summer heat that Joe and I felt it might be better for her to just avoid it. Also, while the dark winter months were hard for her, San Diego is perhaps the southernmost city in the United States and, therefore, receives the most sunlight, and that seemed reasonable to us.

We found a cute little house for Maggie in Ocean Beach. She loved living there. Ocean Beach is a funky, laid-back little beach town, and she fit right in.

I remember that she was worried that the rent was so high—$750 a month. Her father and I had a good laugh about that; heck, at one time in her life, $750 brought us about thirty minutes!

One day, she called, all excited. She had seen a bunch of girls running on the beach, so she ran with them for a while. She found out they went to Point Loma Nazarene University, a private college, and immediately made an appointment with the coach of the cross-country team. I was horrified. I felt college was just too much stress for her and didn't want anything to do with this idea! Regardless, I didn't say anything and privately hoped the interview would not go well.

But of course, it did. The coach remembered her! He sent for her transcripts, checked her eligibility, and told her if she enrolled in a local junior college and got some more credits under her belt, he would see to it that she could enroll at PLNU the next fall. Off she went to the local college, was enrolled, and started in again.

One night at 2:00 a.m., the phone rang. It was Maggie, and she was crying terribly. When we finally calmed her down enough to *speak, she said her stomach hurt. (I was so relieved, I think I actually laughed as I handed the phone over to Joe!) He talked to her for a while, helped her decide on a plan of attack (after all, it was 2:00 a.m., and we lived four hundred miles away). She was to call a cab and go to the local hospital emergency room. After she was examined, she was to call us back so we could figure out what to do. About 4:00 a.m., she called again. The doctors had told her they thought she was just having bad cramps. They made an appointment for her with a doctor there in Ocean Beach for nine that morning, and she thought she could stand it until then. That doctor agreed with the ER docs; he gave her some mild pain pills, and that was the end of that. She said her stomach still hurt—but not as bad, so she went on.*

She had another episode about three weeks later. Lots of pain, another panicked call, another ride to an emergency room, and another "just cramps." Now, I was worried—I reread all my bipolar literature to see if mental problems could bring on physical problems. Little did I know they were definitely related—just not in the way I thought! She had finals coming up and said she had to finish these classes so that she could start in the fall at PLNU, so she did. (She told me later that her stomach felt better if she held her arm across it, so she took her finals one-handed!)

The next week, she called again. This time, Joe and I decided I had to go see what was going on. I drove down, took one look, and took her to another emergency room. This time we did discover what the problem was, but the problem wasn't with Maggie! They took us into an examination room. A doctor came in, asked about her symptoms, poked around on her abdomen, then asked if she was taking any medications. Maggie answered, "Depakote." The hands came up off her stomach, and he left the room. He came back and said she had a bad case of cramps and handed me a prescription. I just sat there absolutely dumbfounded. This was a totally knee-jerk diagnosis. This doctor had decided she was making it up because she was taking a medication for a mental illness!!! I gathered her up and walked her back to the car. I asked her if there was any other hospital she had not yet been to, and she said there was, so we drove there.

This time, I told her not to say anything about the Depakote. We went through the same drill but did not mention her medication. This time, the poking around went on for a while, then they decided to have her drink a solution so they could x-ray her stomach. She kept it down for about twenty minutes and then threw up violently. Now things started to happen quickly; they took her upstairs and used a diagnostic machine to try to see what was going on. Very shortly, I was told that Maggie had a serious problem, and they were going to need to operate as soon as they could locate the surgeon that they wanted to handle the case.

They were certain that her appendix had burst at least seven weeks before—the night of the first attack! After the operation, the surgeon came out and talked to me. He told me that Maggie's appendix had formed a sac around the break and that her immune system just went into overdrive to contain the infection. The appendix and this sac had ended up about the size of a small orange. He told me that he used to see similar cases years ago when the fishing boat captains leaving San Diego harbor all carried penicillin to use if anyone on the boat came down with appendicitis.

The boats could not come back in—but by giving the sick seaman the penicillin, their bodies could fight the infection until the boat docked again. He told me one more thing, which I will never forget. He said that someone must have been watching over her and that there must be something that she was supposed to do in this life. Again, I thought of those mysterious ways.

So the thing I had been so frightened of for so long had almost happened; the mental illness had almost killed her—but with a twist! It was other people's perception—no, even worse, medical personnel's perception of what she was, a mentally ill person—that almost caused her death. I still just shake to think about it.

She convalesced most of the summer. She had to wait six weeks to begin running again, and she was continually concerned about being ready to join the cross-country team at PLNU. She had finished all the required classes, however, so the coach was true to his word and helped her be admitted. She had to pick a major since she was finally a sophomore, so she picked psychology— and she finally had a team again.

She had a hard time running. It wasn't the easiest thing in the world anymore; in fact, it was hard work. She didn't enjoy it at all. I suggested that perhaps it was time to call it a day, but she said she had promised the coach, and she would keep her promise. The race season started, but she didn't call to tell us how she had done, so I didn't push. About halfway through the season, she had a race in Fresno—back on the old course that she had torn up as a teenager— so I asked her old coach from high school, Mr. Roeber, if he would like to go with me to see her run. He said he would and that he would meet me there. When the race began, and as they all tore out of sight, I could not help but remember that awful day three years before, which was the last time I had seen Maggie run. When the finishers began to come in, and Maggie wasn't with them, I realized then that I might be watching her last race too. Her whole team came in, and still no Maggie. She was one of the stragglers, running heavily, struggling with every step. I turned to her coach, and like me, he had tears in his eyes. I knew we were both remembering the gazelle she had been.

At the same time, I was never prouder of her; she could have quit at any time, but quitting had never been her strong suit. (I feel *that this particular quality has helped her throughout her whole life and will probably be the most important quality that sees her through whatever challenges lay ahead. She simply is not the quitting kind!)*

Amy's View - My Last Thoughts

My sister inspires me to be a better person. I try to keep courage in front of her at all times. This is her life. She has to take her medication. As much as she would like to just "take a vacation from this illness," it is always there every morning; and it means so much to me that she is willing to just get up and fight anyway. I hope to keep helping in the little ways—taking my niece to the beach so Mags can catch up on her sleep or wading through laundry if it starts to breed in the laundry room. In short, I know I can't be in that boxing ring, but I can surely be hanging in her corner with the towel, ready with my encouragement and love.

Maggie's Mom – After College

She finished the season. Joe and I went to the banquet for the team. She was genuinely appreciated by the rest of the girls. She finished the semester and doggedly started in on the next one. She had no use for her psychology major, but I think she didn't know what else to do.

The next step came as a result of an offhand remark I made to my friend Debra, my hairdresser. I said I was trying to think of a simple career that Maggie could do so she wouldn't have to keep going to college. Debra said she knew just the thing—aesthetician school! I asked what on earth that was, and she said, "Facials!" I looked it up in the library. It sounded good—helping people, between five hundred and six hundred hours of instruction; and to succeed, the practitioner needs a wealthy populace of people who cared about their skin.

This sounded like San Diego to me. I broached the idea to Maggie, and she seemed interested. Two weeks later, she called and asked how we would feel if she just quit college because a session at a local beauty school was starting up right away and there was room for her if she could come. We said, "Of course," and there she was heading in a new direction. What a relief! The next couple of years went flying by. Maggie graduated from aesthetician school and got a job in a spa. She wasn't busy enough and found a nail salon that wanted to expand, and she talked her way into it. Her business got better and better, and she was able to take care of more and more of her own expenses.

Matt had graduated from college and had gotten a job in the San Diego City Schools as a physical education teacher. He also moved to the beach about three blocks from Maggie's little house. He had a dark brown bachelor pad; she had a sunny little house! They surfed and swam and just generally beached it up! Maggie's brain settled down to a reliable rhythm: a bit down in the fall—but not too much down anymore, and a little up in the spring—but not too much up anymore.

We had reached a milestone that I had heard about six years before—a milestone that had seemed totally out of reach at the time. In my quest to find out about bipolar disorder, I went to a lecture about it, back in the beginning of our trials with Maggie. The doctor stood behind the podium and started his lecture by telling us, "There are about 180 people in this room to hear me lecture about this particular mental illness. I need you to know that you are 180 people who either have bipolar illness or have loved ones who are bipolar—and who have not yet figured out how to live with it! The rest of the people who are bipolar are out at the ball game, hiking, working at their jobs, and living their lives. Your job is to get out there too!" Many a time, when things were darkest, I would *remember that speech and pray that we would find our way back to a life where we had figured out how to live with it.*

And we did it! Maggie and Matt got married. They have a sunny house in San Diego.

Matt and I at our wedding in 2002. (Courtesy the Hurst family)

They have a big yellow dog named Jackson. Three years ago, they made the decision to try to have a baby. My first reaction was horror! And in the very next moment, I reminded myself that it was not my decision, but the decision of two young people who wanted to have a family. Not an easy decision—one that must have taken a long time of agonizing what-ifs, but nevertheless, that was their desire. Maggie had to quit taking her medication for the first time in ten years. Fortunately, she got pregnant immediately, and the pregnancy hormones helped keep her straight for eight and a half months. Ms. Allison Isabelle arrived early and with a bang. We got Maggie's medication started again, but it was a long nine months before she knew up from down. Donna and I took turns staying with the new family. Then, when we were exhausted from caring for a newborn and a "nutty mother," we hired a doula, a Greek term for a grandmother who comes to help the new mother learn how to care for her baby.

We found Ann, a retired navy nurse from Belgium, who came every day and helped our new mother become a real mother to her baby. What a wonderful treasure Ann was—and is! She fell in love with our little family, and Donna and I knew we have at least one more grandmother with a claim on our Allie Belle! Did my life change? Yes, indeed. Besides everything else, I was forced into painting—and have been painting ever since. My work is in many galleries, and my prices are going up.

Because of a painting trip to Italy, I realized the ground at our ranch was the same as the ground in the Mediterranean countries and came home and planted six hundred olive trees. I have a thriving olive oil business that soothes my soul.

My mom, my daughter Allie, me, dad, and Matt. (Courtesy the Hurst family)

I also went into business with a good friend of mine who also had a small cow-calf herd. We sell hormone-free, antibiotic-free beef to our neighbors and customers, and our business is taking off. Last year, we passed the $50,000 figure in sales; so this year, we should start making some actual money! This past year, I planted a three-acre vineyard—and in three years, should have my own red wine to go with the beef and olive oil.

But the biggest change in my life was finding my church. One day, I think I was still driving back and forth to Stanford, I saw my retired Episcopal priest on the street and stopped and asked him to have coffee and talk. He listened to whatever tale of woe was my mantra for the day and told me he was attending a new church and I should come too. I was never particularly religious, and in fact, my prayers during Maggie's illness ran to "Oh, God, why is this happening to me?" But he had called, and I followed him into the Orthodox Church of America. I didn't know why I was there. I liked the people, and I liked that the priest came down to our little community from Sacramento every two weeks; and anyone can go to church once every two weeks!

I liked to sing, and the little choir needed an alto. I liked the icons because they were beautiful and warm and they seemed like company. I learned to paint them—or in the orthodox terminology, "write them." This was such a little church that I knew they needed me, if only for the warm body every Sunday. But I really didn't know why I needed them. I just kept going, until one Sunday, our deacon gave the sermon. He was just beginning to give the homilies—and he was just getting his feet under him. Sometimes, he would lose his train of thought and ramble a bit, and that was when I always just wandered away into my own thoughts right along with him; but this day, one of those mysterious ways came rumbling at me like a freight train!

The deacon was relating the story about the twelve lepers whom Jesus met outside the town. How terribly disfigured they were—how scorned and ridiculed and shunned by all the people they were, and it seemed as if he was talking about Maggie. All of a sudden, I thought about that terrible disease, leprosy—that it really was a lot like being "mentally ill." The people had a normal life, and had normal families, and out of the blue this awful disfigurement struck—and their lives were turned upside down. They were banished from the towns and had to live their lives in agony in any way they could, with no hope of a cure. As the deacon continued the homily, he told how Jesus healed the lepers and told them to go into the temple and offer up prayers, but instead, all but one of them ran home to show their families that they were cured. That's right—all but one, the one who was grateful and went into the temple and gave thanks.

At that moment, I knew why I was there and why I will always be there: I have a place to give thanks. Thanks for a daughter who is strong enough and who will fight for her life enough, thanks for my family who was strong enough to hold each other up while we battled with the "monster that came to dinner," and thanks for God who has worked in such mysterious ways to save us all.

Maggie, Allison and Matt Reese, 2010.

(Courtesy Just Hatched Photography; photograph Melissa Perkins Weisbrod)

AFTERWARD

Now I am thirty-three years old, and yes, it has been a rough road to say the least. But I would not trade anything that I have gone through. I have the most amazing husband and my beautiful two-year-old daughter, Allison Isabelle, and I live in San Diego. I owe the biggest thanks to God. Without God, I would not be here. He made it all possible for me to get through the awful times I have had.

Of course, my mom; my dad; my sister, Amy; my brother, Tom; Carrie; Matt's parents; and most of all, my angel Matt were there to surround me with help.

But when you get right down to it, it is God that was there for me every waking moment. I am now a devout Christian, and I owe my life to Jesus. I hope that for all of you out there that are suffering from bipolar disorder are able to accept a higher power that you can depend on. He will get you through. Go to church and see for yourself. He will make a difference to manage this tough illness.

As for smaller things that get me through day by day there is: going to my doctor, taking my medication, not overdoing my activities even though it is so hard to do, yoga to relax my body, walking out in the sunshine, writing in my journal, talking to friends and family about my emotions, and most of all, not being afraid to tell the world that I have a mental illness.

You might have noticed that other voices in my book are all women's voices—my mom, my sister, my best friend, and my mother-in-law. None of the men in my life felt the need to write something. But after thinking about my husband, my dad, my brother, and my father-in-law, I realize that they have done just exactly what they do best—they put their head down and go to work to fix, if they can, whatever problem comes up for me. Their support is just something I can count on no matter what happens. They don't obsess about things, they don't endlessly discuss my problems, they don't constantly suggest new directions—they just love me. How absolutely wonderful! I love my life and look forward to every day ahead with Matt and Allie. I wish all of you the best whether you are bipolar, have a family member who is ill, or have a friend that needs you.

ACKNOWLEDGMENTS

My sincerest thanks and gratitude to:

Jim Roeber, for his guidance and coaching which inspired my running career.

Chuck Brewster, for being my biggest fan.

Susan and John Russel, for believing in the book and being the first to put Runaway Mind in a bookstore, The Mountain Bookshop.

T. A. Jacobs, for all his help in the beginning of the book project and devoted prayers.

Anne Cavagnaro, for not only being a fantastic math teacher but coming to visit me in the mental hospital when I was so ill.

Angie Andreason Phillips, for befriending me during my darkest times at The University of Idaho.

Andra Simmons, for always telling me the "pit of hell" would go away someday and inspired me to write.

Clairemont Covenant Church, my church family, for being there for me 100%.

Tara Lazo, for friendship and insight.

Bryan Tarr, for his tenacity and determination in social media.

Ellen Stiefler, a hard working agent whose dynamic vision gave this project direction, focus and life.

Dr. James Reese, for always running interference and never giving up in which a way he could help.

Dr. Linda Garfield, the best psychiatrist at Stanford, for starting me back to the road to recovery.

Donna Reese, for her love, compassion, and prayers.

Carrie Webber, a loyal best friend that never gave up on me no matter how awful things got.

Tom Hurst, my brother, who always loves me and is there with a hug.

Amy Hurst Kownacki, a sister I love to pieces who stuck with me through thick and thin.

Leslie Hurst, my mother, who didn't take no for an answer, and who would do anything and give up anything to save me.

Joe Hurst, my father, for always taking my calls day or night and saving my life more times than I can count.

APPENDICES

RECOMMENDATIONS FOR RECOVERY

Appendix A

The Maggie Minute - Ten Assessment Questions

(with thanks to National Alliance on Mental Illness by NAMI Michigan for these helpful points. See www.nami.org)

1. Have you lost interest in your daily activities? Have you lost your energy? Are you excessively tired?

2. Have you lost your appetite or lost weight, or has your appetite increased and you've gained weight?

3. Do you feel hopeless, worthless, or guilty to a degree that reaches unreasonable and delusional proportions?

4. Do you think about death or about harming yourself, or do you wish you were dead, or have you attempted suicide?

5. Do you have a decreased need for sleep? Do you have boundless energy, enthusiasm or activity? Are you not sleeping as well as you usually do? Are you sleeping too little or too much?

6. Are you short tempered or argumentative? Do you have explosive outbursts of irritable mood or behavior?

7. Is your speech rapid, loud or disorganized?

8. Are you feeling euphoric, irritable or expansive?

9. Do you engage in activities which have painful consequences, such as spending sprees, reckless driving, hyper-sexuality?

10. Do you have delusional thinking?

Appendix B

Bipolar disorder is a serious medical illness for which a sufferer should see a doctor. Follow your doctor's orders above all. The following suggestions are things that I do over and above taking my medicine and following my doctor's instructions. I hope they help you as they've helped me.

The Maggie Minute - Ten Assessment Questions

1. Take a 15 minute walk.

2. Have lunch with a friend.

3. Go on a car ride with a friend or family member.

4. Get out of bed, take a hot shower, brush your teeth and put clothes on.

5. Have a good cry...get it out!

6. Get 8 hours of sleep.

7. Do a project. Mine is restoring furniture.

8. Watch a funny movie

9. Get a change of scenery. Mind is the ocean. I love collecting sea glass.

10. Journal even your worst thoughts on paper. It gets it out.

Appendix C

Bipolar disorder is a serious medical illness for which a sufferer should see a doctor. Follow your doctor's orders above all. The following suggestions are things that I do over and above taking my medicine and following my doctor's instructions. I hope they help you as they've helped me.

The Maggie Minute - Ten Assessment Questions

1. Sleep is key. I need 10 plus hours per night to function well.

2. Take time to eat...I tend to forget. Remembering to eat is so important, otherwise anger issues arrive.

3. Swimming makes my brain relax.

4. When you get angry, take a walk until you can calm down.

5. Limit your schedule. Don't take on too much. It will only put you back weeks or months.

6. Get a Massage, or your nails or hair done. This makes me stay still and calms down my brain.

7. Scream and cuss at the trees – they won't get injured!

8. Play music. I play guitar, piano, and sing in the shower and the car.

9. Go on an outing with a friend to a place that is calming. My special places are the ocean or a mountain lake.

10. Garden. I take it out on the weeds!

You will find inspiration and hope for living with Bipolar Disorder by visiting me at:

Facebook: https://www.facebook.com/RunawayMind

Blog: http://chicwildmamma.blogspot.com

Twitter: http://twitter.com/RunawayMindBook

Website: http://www.runawaymind.com

YouTube: http://www.youtube.com/user/runawaymindbook

Send Maggie Reese an email at runawaymind@gmail.com with any questions or share your story of inspiration.

Sign up for Maggie's newsletter, The Maggie Minute, at RunawayMind.com

To contact us and/or order additional copies of "Runaway Mind, My Own Race with Bipolar Disorder" email us at Publisher@TransmediaBooks.com or write us at 360 Nueces Street, Suite 2405, Austin, Texas 78701 TransmediaBooks.com.

TRANSMEDIA BOOKS and colophon are trademarks of Transmedia Multiverse, LLC

For information regarding special discounts for bulk purchases, please contact Transmedia Books Special Sales at 1-858-756-5767 or sales@TransmediaBooks.com.

TRANSMEDIA BOOKS

360 Nueces Street, Suite 2405

Austin, Texas 78701

Manufactured in the United States of America

Library of Congress Control Number: 2012944261

ISBN-13: 978-0-9858861-1-0

Made in the USA
San Bernardino, CA
05 November 2018